you be sweet

You Be Sweet

Sharing Your Heart One Down-Home
Dessert at a Time

PATSY CALDWELL and AMY LYLES WILSON

THOMAS NELSON

Since 1798

NASHVILLE   DALLAS   MEXICO CITY   RIO DE JANEIRO

Published in Nashville, Tennessee, by Thomas Nelson. Thomas Nelson is a registered trademark of Thomas Nelson, Inc.

Photography by Ron Manville

Food Styling by Teresa Blackburn

Photos on pages 24, 186, and 222 are from Fotolia.com

Thomas Nelson, Inc., titles may be purchased in bulk for educational, business, fund-raising, or sales promotional use. For information, please e-mail SpecialMarkets@ThomasNelson.com.

Library of Congress Cataloging-in-Publication Data

Caldwell, Patsy, 1939–
  You be sweet : sharing your heart one down-home dessert at a time / Patsy Caldwell, Amy Lyles Wilson.
    p. cm.
  Includes bibliographical references and index.
  ISBN 978-1-4016-0173-7 (hardback)
  1. Desserts. I. Wilson, Amy Lyles, 1961– II. Title.
  TX773.C245 2012
  641.86—dc23   2012009400

Printed in the United States of America

12 13 14 15 16 QG 6 5 4 3 2 1

To the memory of my father, Hayden Foster. He loved sweets, and because of that, we had dessert with every meal. Also, to my brothers and sisters, Edward, Elizabeth, Jr., Louise, Juanita, Tess, Don, and Billy.

PATSY CALDWELL

In honor of my sisters, Ann Holifield and Ginny Mounger, and my husband, Henry Dennis Granberry III, who have taught me, through food and other means, what it means to be a family.

AMY LYLES WILSON

CONTENTS

INTRODUCTION

"You be sweet," my mother said to me as long ago as 1967, when I was six years old and heading off to my first day of school at Hattie Casey Elementary. She uttered those same words as recently as last week when I left her at the retirement home in Mississippi where she lives to drive the four hundred miles back to my home in Tennessee. Like generations of other Southerners, that phrase has served my family well for decades, regardless of the occasion. Mother practically raised my two sisters and me on those three little words, along with "be careful," "mind your manners," and "always wear a slip." No doubt her own mother offered similar instruction to her when she was growing up as the only daughter in a family of three sons in rural Mississippi in the 1920s and 1930s.

The all-purpose phrase saw me through my childhood: "You be sweet," Mother advised as I went next door to jump on a neighbor's trampoline; "You be sweet," she said when I told her the clique in junior high wanted little to do with me; "You be sweet," she repeated when, in my twenties, I relocated to a town where I knew nary a soul; and now, "You be sweet," she says as we hang up the phone from our long-distance calls.

You might be led to think I wasn't a nice person, as often as Mother has encouraged me to "be sweet." And if she trotted out the harsher translation, "Don't be ugly"—not to be interpreted, as it was by a friend who's not from around here, as a demand to look pretty—I knew I had better watch my step. Surely I was overreacting when someone was rude to me at school, wasn't I? Didn't I want the best for the person who was promoted over me at work despite my seniority?

But I dare say I grew up as decent and civilized as the next girl in the Deep South, born to a culture crammed full of tradition, hospitality, and decorum. It's what we say, like "bless your heart" and "y'all come back." It's also how we live. These customs are such a part of me that I can't imagine not having the terms in my lexicon. I even catch myself telling the dog, Hiram, to "be sweet" when I leave him alone in the house. What I really mean, I suppose, is "Don't chew up the furniture," but that's not what flows from my mouth. I say it to my husband when he's on his way to the driving range, unlikely to interact with another human being for two solid hours (which, if the truth be known, is his preference).

There are myriad ways to "be sweet," of course, such as volunteering at the homeless shelter, remembering Aunt Carlisle's birthday, and writing thank-you notes. And then there is food: baking a pie for a new neighbor, icing a cake for a co-worker who is ill, or mixing up a batch of brownies for a family gathering. As with *Bless Your Heart: Saving the World One* *Covered Dish at a Time,* Patsy Caldwell and I invite you to consider that the recipes in *You Be Sweet* are about more than food. We like to think they present opportunities for connection and community, and we hope they inspire you to serve up a piece to others as an expression of welcome, sympathy, celebration, or concern. For we believe that the sharing of food is akin to the sharing of one's heart, and we can think of no better way for us to "be sweet" to one another.

Amy Lyles Wilson

Chapter 1

SIP AND SEE
THE BABY

Back in Ida's day, women had babies without making a fuss or calling attention to themselves. They simply got married, got pregnant—in that order—and ran an announcement in the local paper heralding the child's arrival. Maybe some friends at church hosted a tasteful shower in the fellowship hall, with punch and an ice ring of frozen fruit. Quite possibly, there were pastel-colored mints in glass bowls and a sheet cake with roses. The gifts were practical, like cloth diapers and handmade bibs. But there were no printed invitations, no party favors, and certainly no games requiring you to drink punch out of a sippy cup. The more experienced mothers wished you well and offered you sound advice. Then you went home, wrote your thank-you notes, and got down to the business of raising your young one as best you could.

Of course, baby showers aren't the only societal norm that has changed since Ida was young. Take television, for instance. For the life of her, Ida can't figure out why people seem to be fascinated by something called "reality TV." Surely their own lives should be interesting enough without needing to spend countless hours watching strangers try to outwit one another on an island or housewives fight over one another's husbands. And Ida has yet to comprehend exactly what the Internet is or why everyone under fifty needs to check something called "e-mail" constantly. Her own grandchildren are glued to their cell phones every time they visit her. Sometimes Ida

wonders why they bother to come at all, but she knows the answer to that in her heart of hearts: Ida raised her daughter, Claire, right. So Claire knows that it's proper to bring the grandchildren to visit their grandmother. And she does, every two weeks like clockwork.

All Ida can do is shake her head when she thinks back to Claire's first pregnancy. Even before she was showing, Claire hired a childbearing coach and signed up for seminars about raising confident children. It wasn't long before she circulated petitions calling for the town council to provide a breastfeeding station in the library and organized community workshops on how to prepare organic baby food. Eventually Claire parlayed her maternal knowledge and enthusiasm into a top-rated mommy blog. Ida has no idea what a blog is, she's sorry to say, but she knows it provides Claire with a sense of accomplishment and purpose. For that, Ida is grateful.

Ida tries to be a hip grandmother, really she does, but sometimes today's world threatens to get the best of her. She'd never heard of a "gender reveal party," for example, until her granddaughter Mallory, Claire's middle child, became pregnant. Ida was actually somewhat scandalized to think that people would know the baby's gender before it arrived. Whatever happened to being surprised? Bless their hearts; these young people today want to have everything figured out before they even get started. *Where's the fun in that,* wonders Ida.

Now there is to be something called a "sip

'n' see" for Mallory and her infant son. Despite Ida's best efforts to appear "with it," she hasn't a clue as to the purpose of the event. She just knows Claire and Mallory expect her to attend, and she doesn't like to disappoint her family.

"Basically it's just friends and family gathering to 'ooh' and 'ahh' over how cute the baby is," says Claire when Ida calls to inquire.

"There's always lots of good food," Claire continues. "Maybe you could bring your strawberry bread pudding? It's Mallory's favorite."

Food is something Ida can relate to, and to her mind it's one of the few things that can stand the test of time and unite young people with old across the generations. Everyone likes to eat, regardless of how newfangled the world has become. Now that Claire has inspired Ida with the thought of taking a dessert to the "sip 'n' see," Ida goes to the pantry and takes out the tin box that contains her most cherished recipes, those scribblings from another era that offer more than mere instruction to Ida; they provide connection, and allow Ida an excuse to revisit some of her fondest memories.

Ida doesn't really need to read the index card telling her how to make strawberry bread pudding, but just holding it in her hands takes her straight to the summers of her childhood when she would spend two weeks with her own grandmother in South Carolina. Their days would start early, maybe with a walk around the farm, before gathering in the kitchen to make sour cream blueberry pancakes with cinnamon honey syrup. It was there that Ida learned to cook.

During those simpler times, back when all Ida had to worry about was eating her vegetables and minding her manners, she also learned what it meant to be family. More than once Ida saw her grandmother preparing food for Aunt Rae, who was always coming down with one ailment or another. As Ida grew, she realized that Aunt Rae was a raging hypochondriac and, if the truth be told, a tad lazy. But that didn't stop Ida's grandmother from helping a loved one. And when it was time for the annual family reunion, Ida's grandmother would bake for days in anticipation: pies, pound cakes, you name it. This was back before there were microwaves and artificial sweetener and global warming. My, how Ida longs for the old days.

But she is not one to stop progress either, so Ida snaps herself back to the present and collects the ingredients for Mallory's favorite dessert. As she gets out her mixing bowl and measuring cup, she reminisces about her own experience as a new mother, savoring both the joy and the challenges of that tender time.

The next day, Ida is heartened to learn that hers is not the only homemade offering at the "sip 'n' see." Sure, there are a few store-bought items on the table, but not an alarming number. (Ida has a nose for such things.) *Maybe there's hope for this generation, after all,* she thinks as she helps herself to a pink lemonade cupcake. By the time Ida starts on her second glass of mint tea and savors another bite of nectarine crumble, she is reassured that Mallory and her friends will do just fine as they make their way in the world.

CARROT CUPCAKES WITH ORANGE CREAM CHEESE ICING

2 cups all-purpose flour
1/2 teaspoon salt
1 teaspoon cinnamon
4 large eggs
1 cup sugar
1 cup vegetable oil
2 cups carrots, finely grated
1 cup apple, finely grated
2/3 cup chopped walnuts
1/2 cup raisins (optional)

Orange Cream Cheese Icing
1/2 cup butter, softened
1 (8-ounce) package cream cheese, softened
1 pound powdered sugar
2 tablespoons orange juice
2 teaspoons orange zest

To make the cupcakes: Preheat the oven to 350 degrees. Place paper liners in two 12-cup cupcake pans.

Mix the flour, salt, and cinnamon together in a small bowl and set aside. In a large mixing bowl, whisk together the eggs, sugar, and oil until well blended. Fold in the grated carrots, grated apples, chopped walnuts, and raisins. Fill each cup 2/3 full. Bake 18 to 20 minutes, or until a toothpick inserted in the center comes out clean. Cool completely and ice.

To make the icing: In the bowl of an electric mixer, beat the butter and cream cheese together until very smooth. Gradually beat in the powdered sugar until fully mixed. Beat in the orange juice and orange zest. Ice the tops of each cupcake.

Makes 24 cupcakes

CHOCOLATE SPOONS

These sure are fun for coffee lovers, and they also make wonderful gifts.

1 cup semi-sweet chocolate chips
16 heavy plastic spoons
1/2 cup white chocolate chips

Place the semi-sweet chocolate chips in a microwave-safe bowl. Heat on high and stir at 10-second intervals until melted. Prepare a baking sheet with wax paper. Dip the spoons in the chocolate. Place on the waxed paper and refrigerate for 1 hour, until firm.

Place the white chocolate chips in a microwave-safe bowl. Heat on high and stir at 10-second intervals until melted. Dip the lower half of the chocolate spoons into the white chocolate. Place on the waxed paper and refrigerate until set. Serve with coffee.

Makes 16 spoons

HOT SPICED COFFEE

This is a fun drink mix to take as a hostess gift. Place in a nice jar, along with a few of the chocolate spoons, and you will have given a gift that someone will enjoy many times over.

2 1/2 cups instant coffee granules, regular or decaffeinated
2 1/2 cups powdered nondairy coffee creamer
1 1/2 cups hot cocoa mix
1 1/2 cups sugar or sugar substitute
1 teaspoon cinnamon
1/2 teaspoon ground cloves

Mix the instant coffee, creamer, and cocoa mix in a blender. Blend until the mixture becomes a powdery consistency. Pour into a large container, and mix with the sugar, cinnamon, and cloves, stirring to combine. Store in an airtight container. When ready to serve, pour 1 cup boiling water into a cup, and add 1 1/2 tablespoons (2 if you like your coffee strong) of the dry mix. Stir to dissolve.

Makes 64–80 cups when mixed with water

"Sip 'n' See" Punch

This is a very pretty punch. It will be perfect to serve when you are showing off your new baby or grandbaby.

Ice Ring
2 cups fresh strawberries, stems attached
1 liter ginger ale

Punch
1 (12-ounce) can frozen orange juice concentrate, thawed

1 (12-ounce) can frozen lemonade concentrate, thawed
1 (46-ounce) can pineapple juice
1 (2-liter) bottle ginger ale
1/2 teaspoon almond extract
1 (1.5-quart) container pineapple sherbet

To make the ice ring: Arrange the strawberries in a ring mold stem side down. Add 1 cup ginger ale and freeze. Add the remaining 3 cups ginger ale and freeze overnight.
To make the punch: Combine the orange juice concentrate, lemonade concentrate, pineapple juice, ginger ale, and almond extract in a large punch bowl, stirring slightly. Scoop the sherbet in. Remove the ice ring from the mold and float it in the punch.

Makes 30 servings

Graham Cracker Crust

1 1/2 cups graham cracker crumbs
1/3 cup powdered sugar
1/2 cup butter, melted

Preheat the oven to 300 degrees. Mix the graham cracker crumbs, powdered sugar, and melted butter together. Press firmly into a 9-inch pie tin. Bake 8 to 10 minutes.

COCONUT BUTTER CRUST

This crust is great for cream pies.

2 tablespoons butter, softened
1 1/2 cups flaked coconut

Preheat the oven to 300 degrees. Spread the butter evenly on the bottom and sides of a 9-inch pie tin. Sprinkle the coconut on top and press it evenly into the butter. Bake 15 minutes or until golden brown.

TOFFEE BARS

When my children found out I was doing a dessert cookbook, both asked if this recipe was going in the book. It was a favorite for them both growing up, and they still enjoy them today.

1 cup butter, softened
1 cup sugar
1 large egg, separated
2 cups all-purpose flour
1 teaspoon cinnamon
1 cup chopped pecans
1 cup semi-sweet chocolate chips, melted

Preheat the oven to 275 degrees. Grease a 13 x 9 x 1-inch baking pan.

In a 2-quart mixing bowl, add the butter, sugar, and egg yolk. Stir to mix well. Add the flour and cinnamon, stirring to incorporate the dry ingredients. Spread into the prepared pan. Brush with the egg white (not whipped). Sprinkle the pecans over the top, pressing into the dough. Bake 1 hour. Remove and drizzle with the melted chocolate chips. Cut while still hot.

Makes 24 bars

GRANNY ERA'S COOKIES

Granny Era Sullivan was known far and wide for these cookies. Her lovely daughter, my friend Bessie Larkins, was kind enough to share the recipe with me.

1 cup butter, softened
1 cup sugar
1 cup brown sugar
1 large egg
1 tablespoon vanilla extract
1 cup vegetable oil
1 cup quick-cooking oats
1 cup pecans, chopped
1 cup flaked coconut
3 ½ cups all-purpose flour
1 teaspoon baking soda
1 teaspoon salt

Preheat the oven to 325 degrees. In a large bowl, cream the butter, sugar, and brown sugar together using an electric mixer. Add the egg and vanilla extract, and mix well. Stir in the oil, oats, pecans, and coconut.

In a medium bowl, mix the flour, baking soda, and salt together. Add the dry ingredients to the batter and mix to combine. Pinch a piece of dough. Roll into a 2-inch ball, and flatten with a fork that has been dipped in cold water. Bake 12 minutes on a large ungreased cookie sheet.

Makes 70 cookies

STRAWBERRY JAM BARS

A great alternative to cookies, these bars are also a good use for your homemade strawberry preserves.

1 cup butter, softened, plus enough to butter the pan
1 cup sugar
2 large egg yolks
2 cups all-purpose flour
$1/8$ teaspoon salt
1 cup pecans, chopped
1 cup strawberry preserves
2 tablespoons powdered sugar for dusting

Preheat the oven to 325 degrees. Butter a 9-inch square baking pan.

Cream the butter and sugar together. Add the egg yolks, beating until well mixed. Gradually add the flour and salt. Stir in the pecans. Spread half of the batter into the buttered dish. Spread the preserves on top. Then spread the remaining batter over a 9-inch piece of waxed paper. Turn upside down over the preserves, and peel off the waxed paper.

Bake 55 minutes or until done. Let cool, cut into bars, and sprinkle them with the powdered sugar.

Makes 8 to 10 servings

CANTALOUPE POPSICLES

Other than fresh from the garden, this is my favorite way to enjoy cantaloupe.

$1/2$ cup water
$1/4$ cup sugar
2 tablespoons honey
4 cups peeled, seeded, and chopped cantaloupe
1 tablespoon lemon juice
$1/8$ teaspoon salt

Combine the water, sugar, and honey in a small saucepan. Cook over medium heat until the mixture comes to a boil, stirring until the sugar dissolves. Cool completely.

Pour the syrup into a food processor. Add the cantaloupe, lemon juice, and salt, blending until smooth. Divide the mixture into eight popsicle molds or 3-ounce paper cups. If using paper cups, freeze 2 hours, then insert the sticks. If you have a popsicle freezer, freeze according to the manufacturer's directions. Freeze solid about 6 hours or overnight.

Makes 8 to 10 servings

SOUTHERN BRUSCHETTA

This is great on a Southern party table or at any bridal shower or tea.

1 foot-long loaf baguette, cut into 24 $1/2$-inch-thick slices
$1/2$ cup butter, softened
$2/3$ cup brown sugar, divided
1 teaspoon cinnamon
$1/2$ cup peaches, finely chopped
$1/2$ cup strawberries, finely chopped
$1/2$ cup pineapple, finely chopped
1 tablespoon fresh lime juice
4 tablespoons walnuts, finely chopped

Preheat the oven to broil. Lay the baguette slices on a large baking sheet.

In a small bowl, mix the butter, $1/3$ cup brown sugar, and cinnamon together. Spread on one side of each baguette slice. Broil for 1 to 2 minutes or until bubbly. In a small bowl, mix the remaining brown sugar, peaches, strawberries, pineapple, lime juice, and walnuts together. Spoon 1 tablespoon over each baguette slice.

Makes 12 servings

Strawberry Tea Sandwiches

This is perfect for any baby shower. But don't forget it when your grandchildren get old enough to have tea parties. They will love this too.

1 (8-ounce) package cream cheese, softened
$1/3$ cup strawberry-flavored drink powder
$1/4$ cup strawberry preserves
$1/4$ cup walnuts, finely chopped
16 slices of wheat or white bread
2 cups strawberries, thinly sliced
Mint leaves to garnish

In a medium bowl, mix the cream cheese, strawberry drink powder, strawberry preserves, and walnuts. Cut the bread slices with a 2-inch cookie cutter so that each slice provides 3 rounds. Spread each 2-inch round with 2 teaspoons of the cream cheese mixture. Top each with a strawberry slice, and garnish with a mint leaf.

Makes 48 servings

CHOCOLATE CHIP PUMPKIN MUFFINS

This recipe makes a lot of muffins. So when I make these, I keep some at home for us to enjoy and then take some for others to enjoy. There is nothing more satisfying for a Southern cook than sharing what she makes. Thanks, Mary England, for sharing your recipe.

1 1/2 cups vegetable oil
2 cups sugar
4 large eggs
2 cups canned pumpkin
3 cups self-rising flour
2 teaspoons cinnamon
1 cup chocolate chips

Preheat the oven to 350 degrees. Grease or use paper baking cups in three (12-cup) muffin tins.

In a large bowl, mix the oil, sugar, eggs, and pumpkin together. In a medium bowl, mix the flour and cinnamon together. Add the dry mixture to the wet mixture. Stir in the chocolate chips. Fill the muffin cups 2/3 full. Bake 25 to 30 minutes, or until a toothpick inserted in the center of the muffins comes out clean.

Makes 36 servings

Note: The fat in this recipe can be altered by substituting applesauce for half of the oil (3/4 cup oil and 3/4 cup applesauce).

Louise's Chocolate Peanut Coconut Bars

My sister Louise is such a great hostess. She always has a tray of these made for family and friends.

1 1/2 cups graham cracker crumbs
1/2 cup sugar
1/2 cup butter, melted
1 (14-ounce) can condensed milk
2 cups flaked coconut
1 cup milk chocolate chips, melted
1 tablespoon creamy peanut butter

Preheat oven to 350 degrees. Lightly grease a 9 x 9-inch square pan.

In a small bowl, mix the graham cracker crumbs, sugar, and butter. Pat the mixture into the pan. Bake 10 minutes.

In a small bowl, stir together the condensed milk and coconut. Spread over the warm crust. Return to the oven and bake for 15 minutes.

Melt the chocolate chips and peanut butter together in a double boiler over medium heat. When the peanut butter mixture has cooled, spread it over the coconut crust. Chill before cutting.

Makes 12 servings

STRawBeRRy BREaD PUDDING WITH CaRaMeL SaUCE

Some people suggest you use French bread when you make bread pudding. Personally, I prefer good old-fashioned white bread. But this recipe will turn out great with whatever bread you choose.

Bread Pudding

1 (15-ounce) package frozen strawberries, thawed
3 tablespoons cornstarch
3 drops red food coloring
3 large eggs, slightly beaten
3 1/2 cups heavy whipping cream
3/4 cup sugar
3 tablespoons butter, melted

1 teaspoon vanilla extract
1/4 teaspoon salt
4 slices bread, cut in 1/2-inch cubes (about 4 cups)

Caramel Sauce

1 cup heavy whipping cream
1 1/2 cups sugar
1 tablespoon butter

To make the bread pudding: Preheat the oven to 350 degrees. Lightly grease an 11 x 9-inch baking dish. In a small saucepan, combine the undrained strawberries and cornstarch. Cook and stir over medium heat until the mixture thickens and bubbles. Stir in the food coloring. Spread the mixture evenly in the baking dish.

In a medium bowl, combine the eggs, cream, sugar, butter, vanilla, and salt. Add the bread cubes, and stir to moisten. Carefully pour the custard mixture over the strawberries. Bake 45 to 50 minutes. Serve warm with caramel sauce.

To make the caramel sauce: Pour the heavy cream into a small saucepan and heat over medium until bubbles form around the edges. Turn the heat to low and keep the cream warm while you prepare the sugar.

Place the sugar in a 10-inch iron skillet over medium heat, stirring constantly with a wooden spoon. When the sugar looks golden and all the sugar is dissolved, stir 30 seconds more. Remove from the heat, and carefully stir in the hot heavy cream. (If the cream is heated, it blends into the sugar better.) Stir in the butter. Cool slightly before serving.

Makes 8 to 10 servings

NECTARINE CRUMBLE

Nectarines come in earlier than peaches usually do. This is a great dessert to make when the peaches aren't ripe yet and you are eager to eat something sweet with that same summer taste.

8 large ripe nectarines, unpeeled and sliced
2 tablespoons plus 3/4 cup butter, divided
1 1/4 cups sugar, divided
2 tablespoons water
1 1/2 cups all-purpose flour
3/4 cup brown sugar
1 cup oatmeal
1/2 teaspoon cinnamon
1/8 teaspoon salt
1/2 cup sliced almonds (optional)

Preheat the oven to 350 degrees. Grease a 13 x 9-inch baking dish.

Place the sliced nectarines, 2 tablespoons butter, 1/2 cup sugar, and water in a medium saucepan. Cover and bring to a boil. Reduce the heat and cook for 10 minutes, stirring occasionally.

While the nectarine mixture is cooking, dice 3/4 cup butter. Combine the flour, 3/4 cup sugar, brown sugar, oatmeal, butter, cinnamon, salt, and almonds in the bowl of an electric mixer. Using the paddle attachment, mix on low speed until the butter is pea-size and the mixture is crumbly.

Pour the nectarines into the prepared baking dish. Sprinkle the crumble mixture evenly on top. Bake 30 to 35 minutes, or until the top is golden brown. Serve warm.

Makes 12 servings

POUND CAKE WITH BLUEBERRY BUTTER

This blueberry butter is great to serve if the new baby is a boy.
You can also use strawberry butter if the baby is a girl.

Pound Cake

4 large eggs, separated
1 1/3 cups sugar, divided
1/2 cup vegetable shortening
1/2 cup butter, softened
1 teaspoon vanilla extract
1/2 teaspoon salt
1 1/2 cups all-purpose flour
1/4 cup light whipping cream

Blueberry Butter

1/2 cup butter, softened
1/3 cup blueberry preserves

To make the pound cake: Preheat the oven to 325 degrees. Grease and flour a 9 x 5-inch loaf pan. In a medium bowl, whip the egg whites on high speed with an electric mixer until soft peaks form. Gradually add 1/3 cup sugar. Set aside. In a large bowl, add the remaining 1 cup sugar with the shortening and butter. Cream at medium speed with an electric mixer until well mixed. Add the vanilla, salt, and egg yolks, and continue to beat for about 3 minutes. Reduce the mixer to low speed, and add the flour and cream, alternately, beginning and ending with the flour.

Pour into the prepared pan. Bake 1 hour and 10 minutes until golden brown, or until a cake tester inserted in the center comes out clean. Let cool in the pan for 10 minutes before removing to a cooling rack. Cool completely before serving. To serve, slice into 1/2-inch thick slices, then again into finger slices. Top with blueberry butter.

To make the butter: In a small bowl, stir the butter and blueberry preserves together. Serve with the pound cake.

Makes 12 servings

CHOCOLATE CUPCAKES WITH PEANUT BUTTER FROSTING

I don't think there are two things much better together than peanut butter and chocolate.

Cupcakes	*Peanut Butter Frosting*
1/2 cup butter, softened	1 1/2 cups powdered sugar
1 cup sugar	1 cup peanut butter
1 teaspoon vanilla extract	1 teaspoon vanilla extract
4 large eggs	1/4 cup heavy whipping cream
1 1/4 cups all-purpose flour	1/4 cup butter, softened
3/4 teaspoon baking soda	
1 1/2 cups chocolate-flavored syrup	

To make the cupcakes: Preheat the oven to 350 degrees. Paper-line two 12-cup muffin tins. Cream the butter, sugar, and vanilla until light and fluffy. Add the eggs, one at a time, beating well after each addition. In a small bowl, combine the flour and baking soda. Alternately add the flour mixture and chocolate syrup to the creamed mixture, beginning and ending with the flour. Pour the batter into the paper-lined muffin cups, filling 2/3 full. Bake 20 to 25 minutes.

Cool for 10 minutes in the pan. Remove to a cooling rack to cool completely before frosting.

To make the frosting: Place the powdered sugar, peanut butter, vanilla, heavy cream, and butter in a large bowl. Beat with an electric mixer at medium speed until smooth. Frost the cooled chocolate cupcakes.

Makes 24 servings

Chapter 2

❧⚬—⚬❧

SWEET GEORGIA VISITS
HER MOTHER

Rosemary Adeline Mitchell didn't plan on being the youngest widow out at Happy Trails Retirement Village. But she's always been one to make the best of even the most troublesome situation, so she is taking things in stride. And although she's not proud of the designation, necessarily, she realizes that Happy Trails is one of the few places where being in your mid-seventies is considered a plus.

Rosemary would be hesitant to admit it—she is nothing if not humble—but the more eligible elderly men often seek after her as a dinner companion. By "more eligible," she means they are able to cut their own food and, more likely than not, to stay awake through dessert. Another advantage of her youth is that Rosemary can still drive a car. She dreads the time when her children approach her about giving up the keys, but that's a worry for another day. Today Rosemary has a full calendar. Her daughter Georgia is coming over, and Rosemary has only an hour to run a few errands, seeing as how she let half the morning get away from her while listening to her neighbor Mildred prattle on about her frustration with her new hearing aids. Her son made her get them, you see, and she can't take hold of the tiny batteries.

"He thinks he's done me a favor," says Mildred. "Meanwhile, I can't hear a thing!"

Georgia is Rosemary's favorite, but please don't let on to the other children. Rosemary is diplomatic enough not to show her favoritism, but it's true that she slips Georgia a twenty-dollar bill now and again. Georgia doesn't need the money—praise God—seeing as how her husband makes a good living selling insurance. But Georgia always accepts the money graciously and puts it in her purse, vowing to donate it to a worthy cause. So far she's contributed to the animal shelter, the food bank, and the drive to get new band uniforms for Luckettville High.

Georgia drops by Happy Trails once every week or so for coffee, and Rosemary is happy to announce that they've come a long way since that first fateful Saturday when her baby girl, now fifty, showed up bearing cinnamon rolls—from the grocery store.

For the life of her, Rosemary cannot tell you why her daughter thought for one minute she could pass off store-bought as homemade. For even though the rolls were on a glass plate, sitting atop a paper doily, Rosemary sensed their imposter status the minute Georgia peeled back the aluminum foil. Rosemary wasn't born yesterday, after all. In fact, she was born in 1938. Choking down a bite of the processed, slightly stale offering, Rosemary realized it was time to admit that even in light of all Georgia's fine qualities—of which there are many, Rosemary wants you to know—the child couldn't cook to save her life.

"Follow me," said Rosemary.

Because Georgia was the only Mitchell child who always did as she was told, she walked behind her mother, silently, as they made their way into the kitchen. It wasn't the kitchen of Georgia's childhood, where their family gathered for supper around the table that Georgia's father had built out of pine. There was no hanging pot rack, no hutch full of apple blossom plates. Gone were the handprints of young children on the refrigerator. Instead, the kitchen was smaller, galley style, with no room to spare. But Rosemary could still make magic there.

After several intense mother-daughter cooking sessions—whatever you do, don't ask about the exploding prune cake—Rosemary had Georgia cutting butter into flour like a pro. Soon they were sporting matching aprons and exchanging recipes.

On the rainy Saturday morning when Georgia showed up at Rosemary's with a pan of gooey sticky buns made from scratch, Rosemary thought she'd been given the keys to the kingdom.

"Perfect," said Rosemary, wiping a drop of icing from her upper lip. "I couldn't have done better myself."

Several weeks later, when Georgia came bearing rice pudding, Rosemary started to cry.

"My mother made this for me whenever I was sick," Rosemary said. "She would bring it to me in bed, warm, in a Mason jar."

Rosemary was so overcome she didn't even notice that Georgia had brought her rice pudding in a plastic container suitable for both dishwasher and microwave. She was too busy telling Georgia stories about the old days in rural Mississippi. How she hadn't known what to expect when her father took her hand and led her down the wooden sidewalk toward a neighbor's house to listen to something called a "radio" for the first time. Or about the late afternoon on the porch swing with her

first beau, a man who would be killed overseas within weeks of that visit. It was as if the rice pudding had somehow launched Rosemary back in time.

As her daughter got ready to leave, Rosemary reached out to squeeze Georgia's cheeks. (It's true. She really did this.)

"I can't believe my baby has so much gray hair," said Rosemary as she tucked a stray strand behind Georgia's left ear.

Rosemary was smart enough to know that Georgia was probably just as shocked to have a mother old enough to be living at Happy Trails. And Rosemary was grateful that instead of making a crack about old age, Georgia simply kissed her mother on her forehead and promised to bring pecan cobbler next time, or maybe buttermilk coconut pie.

"You be sweet," Rosemary said, as way of good-bye, just as she has done since Georgia was a child.

It never occurs to Rosemary that Georgia might worry about a few home-cooked desserts being sufficient reimbursement for all her mother has done for her over the years. From handmade Halloween costumes to piano recitals, ballet lessons to sleepovers, prom dresses and braces to that first used car and college tuition. Not to mention all the pep talks and keeping of confidences along the way.

Like generations of mothers before her, Rosemary isn't looking for credit. She doesn't expect any kind of repayment or acknowledgment for her selfless contribution to Georgia's development. But as long as Georgia shows up at her door bearing baked goods, Rosemary will take, and eat, and give thanks.

CORNbREAD SPIDER CAKE

This is called Spider because of the type of iron skillet it was cooked in many years ago. The skillets had tiny legs on the bottom. This is a breakfast favorite.

2 tablespoons butter
2 large eggs, beaten
2 cups milk, soured with 4 teaspoons vinegar
3/4 cup sugar
3/4 cup yellow cornmeal
1 cup all-purpose flour
1/2 teaspoon salt
1/2 teaspoon baking soda
1 cup heavy whipping cream
Maple syrup, for serving

Preheat the oven to 350 degrees. Melt the butter in a 9-inch iron skillet over medium heat.

Place the beaten eggs in a medium mixing bowl. Add the soured milk to the eggs and set aside. In a large bowl, stir together the sugar, cornmeal, flour, salt, and baking soda. Stirring, slowly add the egg mixture to the dry ingredients. Pour the batter into the hot skillet. Pour the cream into the center of the batter, but do not stir. Bake 45 to 50 minutes, or until the cake is golden brown.

Let sit in the pan for 5 to 10 minutes before cutting into wedges to serve. Serve with maple syrup. This can be served from the skillet.

Makes 10 to 12 servings

PEACH CRISP

The preparation of a crisp and cobbler are quite similar. But I think this is actually easier to make.

3/4 cup pecans, chopped
1/2 cup oats
1/3 cup brown sugar
2/3 cup all-purpose flour, divided
1 teaspoon almond extract
1 1/2 teaspoons cinnamon, divided
1/8 teaspoon salt
3 tablespoons butter
6 cups peeled and sliced peaches
1 1/4 cups sugar

Preheat the oven to 350 degrees. Butter or spray a 13 x 9-inch baking dish.

In a small bowl, combine the pecans, oats, brown sugar, 1/3 cup flour, almond extract, 1/2 teaspoon cinnamon, and salt, stirring to mix. Cut the butter in with your fingers until the mixture is crumbly. Set aside. In a large bowl, toss the peaches with sugar, 1/3 cup flour, and 1 teaspoon cinnamon. Pour into the baking dish. Top with the pecan mix. Bake 40 to 45 minutes or until bubbly and golden brown.

Makes 10 to 12 servings

IRON SKILLET CARAMEL PIE

I would choose this to be the last dessert I eat on this earth. Caramel is my absolute favorite.

Pie

2 cups sugar, divided

$1/2$ cup all-purpose flour

$1/8$ teaspoon salt

2 cups milk

4 large egg yolks, beaten (save the whites for meringue)

2 tablespoons butter

1 (9-inch) pie shell, baked

Meringue

4 large egg whites

$1/2$ teaspoon cream of tartar

$1/2$ cup sugar

To make the pie: Preheat the oven to 350 degrees. Caramelize 1 cup of sugar by placing it in a medium iron skillet over medium heat. Begin stirring with a wooden spoon. The sugar will come together in pieces the size of almonds. Continue to stir until the sugar becomes like syrup and is the color of caramel. While the sugar is heating up, put the remaining 1 cup of sugar, flour, and salt in a large saucepan. Mix well, and gradually add the milk. Add the beaten eggs. Cook over low to medium heat until hot, stirring constantly.

Add the caramelized sugar to the milk, stirring quickly. Cook until thick, continuing to stir. Add the butter, and pour into the pie shell. Top with the meringue and bake for 8 to 10 minutes.

To make the meringue: Beat the egg whites and cream of tartar in the bowl of an electric mixer until soft peaks form. Gradually add the sugar, and continue beating until stiff. Spread the meringue on top of the pie and bake.

Makes 6 to 8 servings

JUST WHAT THE DOCTOR ORDERED: CINNAMON ROLLS WITH VANILLA ICING

I always take these when I have an eye doctor appointment. Recently the young lady who used to work for my eye doctor started working for my medical doctor. When I walked in, she asked if I'd brought cinnamon rolls. Now I have to start taking them to that office too.

Cinnamon Rolls

2 packages active dry yeast

2 teaspoons plus 1 2/3 cups sugar, divided

1/4 cup lukewarm water

3/4 cup milk

1/2 cup butter, softened

1 1/2 teaspoons salt

3 large eggs, slightly beaten

4 cups all-purpose flour, divided

1 tablespoon vegetable oil

1 cup butter, melted and divided

1 tablespoon cinnamon

1 cup pecans, chopped

1 cup raisins, optional

Icing

2 pounds powdered sugar

1 cup butter, softened

2/3 cup light whipping cream

2 teaspoons vanilla extract

To make the cinnamon rolls: Dissolve the yeast, 2 teaspoons of sugar, and water in a small bowl. Let the yeast begin to bubble, about 3 minutes. Combine the milk, softened butter, 2/3 cup sugar, and salt in a small saucepan over low heat. Heat until lukewarm. Pour the milk mixture into a large bowl, and add the yeast, eggs, and 2 cups of flour. Beat on low speed with an electric mixer for about 3 minutes, or until bubbles form. Cover and let set for 30 minutes.

Add the remaining flour and continue to beat until the mixture forms a soft dough and leaves the sides of the bowl; this could take 5 to 8 minutes. Brush the top of the dough with the oil. Cover and let rise until doubled in bulk.

Punch down and place in the refrigerator overnight. When you are ready to make the rolls, divide the dough into 2 equal pieces. Roll on a floured board to a 3/8-inch thick rectangle. Cover the dough with half of the melted butter, cinnamon, 1 cup sugar, pecans, and raisins. Roll up, beginning at the long end, and pinch the seam together. Slice into 1-inch pieces. Place the rolls cut side down in a greased 13 x 9-inch baking pan. Set in a warm place to rise for about 2 hours.

Preheat the oven to 375 degrees. Bake 15 minutes or until golden brown. Cool and cover with icing.

To make the icing: Cream together the powdered sugar, butter, cream, and vanilla with an electric mixer until smooth.

Makes 24 cinnamon rolls

Note: This dough also makes delicious dinner rolls. Use the same process as other rolls, cut into desired shapes, and let rise. You can also exchange the milk in the icing recipe for orange juice.

MoLasses Pecan Pie

The molasses really gives this twist on the traditional pecan pie a distinctive flavor.

4 large eggs
3/4 cup sugar
1/4 cup butter, melted
3/4 cup light corn syrup
1/2 cup molasses
1 cup pecans, chopped
1 teaspoon vanilla extract
1 teaspoon apple cider vinegar
1 (9-inch) deep-dish pie crust, unbaked

Preheat the oven to 400 degrees. In a large mixing bowl, beat the eggs and sugar together. Add the butter, corn syrup, molasses, pecans, vanilla, and vinegar. Stir to mix well. Pour into the pie shell. Bake 10 minutes. Reduce the heat to 300 and continue to cook for 50 minutes or until set in the center. Cool before serving.

Makes 6 to 8 servings

Teacakes

Teacakes have been served in the South since the eighteenth century. They are a lot easier to make today than they were back then. But they taste just as good.

1/2 cup butter, softened
1 cup sugar
2 large eggs, beaten
1 teaspoon vanilla extract
1/3 cup milk
3 cups all-purpose flour, plus additional flour for rolling the dough
2 teaspoons baking powder
1/8 teaspoon salt
1/2 teaspoon nutmeg

Preheat the oven to 350 degrees. Lightly grease a large cookie sheet.

Cream together the butter and sugar in the bowl of an electric mixer. Add the eggs, vanilla, and milk. In a large bowl, mix the flour, baking powder, salt, and nutmeg. Add 1 cup of the dry ingredients to the creamed mixture. Mix until smooth. Stir in the remaining 2 cups of dry ingredients. Chill until firm, about 30 minutes.

Roll out onto a lightly floured board to 1/8-inch thickness. Cut with a 3-inch cookie cutter, rerolling the scraps and continuing to cut until all the dough has been used. Place the dough on the cookie sheet and bake for 12 to 15 minutes or until the edges begin to brown. The cookies will become crisp as they cool.

Makes 36 servings

SOUR CREAM LEMON PIE

Everyone loves a luscious lemon pie. This is a great dessert for a hot summer day.

1 cup sugar
3 tablespoons cornstarch
1/8 teaspoon salt
1/4 cup butter
2 teaspoons grated lemon zest
1/2 cup lemon juice
3 large egg yolks, slightly beaten
1 cup milk
1 cup sour cream
1 (9-inch) pie shell, baked
1 cup heavy whipping cream
2 tablespoons powdered sugar
1/4 cup pecans, chopped and toasted

Combine the sugar, cornstarch, and salt in a medium saucepan. Add the butter, lemon zest, lemon juice, and egg yolks. Gradually stir in the milk, mixing well. Bring to a boil over medium heat, stirring constantly until the mixture is thick. Cool completely and fold in the sour cream. Pour into the pie shell and chill in the refrigerator.

In a medium bowl, beat the whipping cream until soft peaks form. Add the powdered sugar and continue to beat until the cream stands on its own when the mixer is removed. Top the chilled pie with the sweetened whipped cream and sprinkle with the pecans. Keep refrigerated until ready to serve.

Makes 6 to 8 servings

peach cobbler

You can't have summer without a peach cobbler with ice cream on top. It's just not possible in the South.

Pie Crust
2 cups all-purpose flour
1 teaspoon salt
$2/3$ cup shortening
$1/2$ cup milk

Peach Filling
6 cups fresh or frozen peaches, sliced
1 $1/4$ cups sugar
2 tablespoons all-purpose flour

$1/8$ teaspoon salt
$1/2$ teaspoon cinnamon
2 tablespoons butter

Topping for Pie
2 tablespoons sugar
$1/4$ teaspoon cinnamon
2 tablespoons butter

To make the pie crust: Mix the flour, salt, and shortening together until it becomes crumbly. Stir in the milk, and gather the dough into a ball. Flatten into a 6-inch circle, wrap with plastic wrap, and refrigerate for 30 minutes. Roll on a lightly floured board until the dough is slightly larger than your baking pan.

To make the peach filling: Preheat the oven to 400 degrees. Lightly grease an 11 x 9-inch baking pan. Place the peaches, sugar, flour, salt, cinnamon, and butter in a medium saucepan over low heat. Bring to a boil and cook, stirring constantly for 2 minutes. Pour into the prepared pan and top with the pie crust.

To make the topping: Sprinkle the sugar and cinnamon over the crust. Dot with thin slices of butter. Cut 3 slits in the top of the crust. Bake 30 minutes, until the pastry is golden brown and the pie bubbles.

Makes 6 to 8 servings

TRADITIONAL SOUTHERN BLACKBERRY COBBLER

The secret to making good cobbler is the same as making good sweet tea. You add the sugar while the berries are hot, just like you add the sugar to tea when the tea is hot. If this is not how you are making your cobbler, try it. It will make a big difference.

12 cups fresh or frozen berries
$1/2$ cup butter, divided
$1/8$ teaspoon salt
1 $1/2$ cups sugar, divided
Pie crust (see recipe on page 37 for Peach Cobbler)
1 teaspoon cinnamon

Preheat the oven to 400 degrees. Bring the berries, $1/4$ cup butter, and salt to a boil in a large saucepan, stirring occasionally. Stir in 1 $1/4$ cup sugar. Pour in a 13 x 9-inch baking pan. Top with the pie crust pastry.

Dot with $1/4$ cup butter, and sprinkle with $1/4$ cup sugar and cinnamon. Prick the top with a fork. Bake 30 minutes or until golden brown.

Makes 12 servings

FUNERAL PIE

If you don't want to have such a downer name, you can also call this a Raisin Pecan Pie. This was a traditional pie to take when someone died. I think it's too delicious to wait that long, myself.

2 large eggs
1 cup sugar
6 tablespoons butter, melted
$1/4$ cup milk
$1^1/2$ cups raisins
$1/2$ cup pecans, chopped
1 teaspoon vanilla extract
1 (9-inch) pie shell

Preheat the oven to 350 degrees. In a medium mixing bowl, beat the eggs. Gradually add the sugar, butter, and milk. Stir in the raisins, pecans, and vanilla. Mix well. Pour into the pie shell and bake for 45 to 50 minutes or until the center is set. Cool before serving.

Makes 6 to 8 servings

PEPPERMINT ICE CREAM

This is my favorite ice cream to make and serve. It is also delicious on fudge pies.

4 cups milk
1 pound peppermint candy, crushed
2 tablespoons all-purpose flour
$1/2$ cup sugar
$1/4$ teaspoon salt
3 large egg yolks, beaten
2 quarts heavy whipping cream

Heat the milk and candy in a large saucepan until tiny bubbles form around the edge of the pan. In a small bowl, mix the flour, sugar, salt, and beaten egg yolks together. Gradually add the egg mixture to the milk mixture, stirring constantly. Bring to a boil over medium heat and cook for 1 minute. Cool completely. Add the cream and freeze in your ice cream freezer according to the manufacturer's directions.

Makes 1 gallon

OLD FASHIONED SOUTHERN CHESS PIE

Legend has it that chess pie got its name because when people would ask someone what kind of pie it was, they would reply, "Just pie." That is, it was just eggs, sugar, and the rest of the standard pie ingredients. Over the years its name became "Jes Pie," which eventually became "Chess Pie."

1/2 cup butter
1 1/2 cups sugar
1 tablespoon vinegar
1 1/2 tablespoons cornmeal
3 large eggs, slightly beaten
1 teaspoon vanilla extract
1 (9-inch) unbaked pie crust

Preheat the oven to 425 degrees. Melt the butter over low heat in a small saucepan. Add the sugar and stir to combine. Remove from the heat, and add the vinegar, cornmeal, eggs, and vanilla, stirring well. Pour into the crust and bake for 10 minutes. Reduce the temperature to 300 degrees, and bake for an additional 40 to 45 minutes or until the pie is set and golden brown.

Makes 6 to 8 servings

HOT BUTTERED LEMONADE

When I was a little girl, we never went to the doctor until we tried this first. I still take this to friends today when they have colds.

4 $1/2$ cups water
1 cup sugar
2 lemons, thinly sliced
$3/4$ cup lemon juice
2 tablespoons butter

Place the water and sugar in a 2-quart saucepan and bring to a boil. Reduce the heat to medium, and add the lemon slices and lemon juice, stirring until the sugar is dissolved and the mixture is thoroughly heated. Pour into 6 mugs, and top each serving with 1 teaspoon butter. Serve hot.

Makes 6 servings

RICE PUDDING

This is a very "childhoodie" recipe to me. It is also a great way to use leftover rice.

3 large eggs
$2/3$ cup sugar
$1/4$ teaspoon salt
1 teaspoon vanilla extract
3 cups milk, heated to the boiling point
$3/4$ cup cooked rice
$1/2$ teaspoon cinnamon
$1/2$ cup raisins, optional

Preheat the oven to 350 degrees. Butter a 2-quart baking dish.

In a medium mixing bowl, beat the eggs slightly. Add the sugar, salt, and vanilla. Slowly add the hot milk, mixing well. Strain into the buttered baking dish. Add the rice, and sprinkle with cinnamon. Add the raisins if desired. Bake 1 $1/2$ hours, or until a knife inserted in the center comes out clean and the pudding is lightly brown. Serve warm.

Makes 6 servings

PEACH AMBROSIA

Traditionally, ambrosia usually just contains oranges. I love adding the peaches and bananas to give this a new taste.

4 large fresh peaches, peeled and sliced
2 large oranges, peeled and sectioned
1 large banana, sliced
1 tablespoon lemon juice
2 tablespoons flaked coconut, toasted

Combine the peaches, oranges, banana, and lemon juice in a 2-quart serving bowl. Cover and chill for 1 hour. Sprinkle with the coconut before serving.

Makes 6 servings

RHUBARB-STRAWBERRY PIE

On farms in the South, you were considered blessed if you had a "pie plant," which is what we called rhubarb. The plant came up in the spring every year. My family didn't have one, but our neighbors did, and I thought they were the richest people in the world because of it.

1 1/4 cups sugar
1/4 cup all-purpose flour
3 cups rhubarb, sliced
2 cups strawberries, sliced
1 (9-inch) deep-dish pie shell, unbaked
2 tablespoons butter
1 (10-inch) crust to top, unbaked

Preheat the oven to 425 degrees. In a large bowl, mix together the sugar and flour. Toss the rhubarb and strawberries together with the dry mix. Place in the pie crust. Dot with the butter. Top with the remaining crust. Cut slits in the crust for the steam to escape. Bake 10 minutes. Reduce the heat to 350 degrees. Bake 30 to 35 minutes or until the crust is golden brown. Let cool slightly before serving.

Makes 6 to 8 servings

HEIRLOOM BLACK WALNUT PIE

I have been eating black walnuts my whole life. When I was a girl, these were sometimes the only nuts we had to use in making pies, cakes, and candies. I am lucky enough to have several friends with walnut trees, and they keep me pretty well stocked. It is a lot of work to get the meat from a black walnut, but it sure is worth it.

3 large eggs, slightly beaten
1 cup light corn syrup
1 cup brown sugar
1/3 cup butter, melted
1/8 teaspoon salt
1 1/2 cups black walnuts
1 teaspoon vanilla extract
1 (9-inch) pie crust, unbaked

Preheat the oven to 350 degrees. Place the eggs in a medium mixing bowl. Add the corn syrup, brown sugar, butter, salt, walnuts, and vanilla. Mix well. Pour the filling into the pie crust. Bake 1 hour, or until the filling is set and the pie is golden brown. Serve warm.

Makes 6 to 8 servings

Chapter 3

THE LADIES WHO LUNCH

Playing bridge is the highlight of the month for Marian Prentiss. Don't misunderstand; she has a rich social life. There's the women's circle at church, her volunteer position at the library, and a longstanding lunch date every Tuesday with her sister at Parker's Drugstore. They still serve lunch, right across the counter from where Old Man Atkinson—that's what they'd called him even when he was young—doles out the pills. Marian never tires of settling into a booth and ordering a ham sandwich and a cherry soda from the fountain. And several times a year, she is invited to some cultural event or another over at the college. But it is bridge that brings her the most satisfaction. She was still waiting for Miss Hibernia to die so she could have her spot in the Luckettville Learned Ladies Society, but the old lady was defying the odds with alarming success. So when Virginia Tarver invited Marian to join the Uptown Bridge Club—the "Uptowners" for short—she jumped at the chance. Marian's not proud of this, but she still feels a little sting, some forty years after the fact, about not getting a Chi Omega bid in college. She had been a legacy, after all. So she's always on the lookout for another shot at sisterhood.

Marian respects the skill required for bridge, certainly. But more important, to Marian's mind at least, are the friendships that have developed over the years. If you pressed her, Marian would confess that she considers her bridge partners as close to her as her own family. Closer, even. (If you knew Marian's family, you'd understand.)

Marian looks forward to their monthly games with the same sort of excitement one might expect from a child nearing her birthday. Nothing fills her with more joyful anticipation than the Uptowners' end-of-year celebration each May, when they pull out all the stops before taking a break for the summer.

Throughout the year, the women take turns hosting. When they meet at Betty Ann's house, they can count on having frozen strawberry salad and pineapple dump cake. Marian suspects the cake is from Annabelle's Bakery, even though Betty Ann arranges the pieces on her mother's Havilland platter so as to give the appearance she has made the dessert herself. The cake is tasty, though, so Marian doesn't criticize Betty Ann openly for passing off someone else's sweets as her own.

Over at Sarah's, there will be fruit salsa with cinnamon chips, and pecan cobbler. Sometimes she goes all out and makes white chocolate soup, but Sarah really has to be in a good mood for that, and it doesn't happen very often. Not that Marian is one to cast aspersions, mind you, but Sarah is known to be sullen even on the sunniest of days. Marian knows good and well she's not the only one to say so, so don't try to tell her otherwise.

But dear, sweet Virginia Tarver puts the rest of the ladies to shame when it is her turn to host. First, she makes sure her linen napkins are starched just enough to appear proper, but not so stiff as to be rendered ineffective. Try as you might, you won't find a stain or a tear on the perfectly folded squares. Then she brings out her fine china, an assortment of dessert plates unrivaled in all of Luckettville. None of them matches, but it doesn't matter, not at Virginia's table. She has a way of making seemingly odd pieces look like they were destined to be placed next to one another. And always there are fresh flowers, even in the dead of winter. Marian never could figure out how Virginia manages to find peonies year-round.

But it is the food that sets Virginia's table apart from the rest. When Virginia offers to host the May gathering, Marian practically swoons. For she knows that means, at the very least, red velvet cheesecake, strawberries on a cloud, and the apple sorbet Virginia learned to make at the Greenbrier. If they were lucky, it would also mean Virginia's secret recipe rum punch.

The women have tried for years to get Virginia to tell them what is in the enticing elixir, but she is resolute in her refusal to reveal the ingredients. Marian had been raised a teetotaler, so she tries to limit herself to two glasses whenever Virginia serves the punch. But sometimes she simply can't resist and ends up with a wee bit more.

Back when Marian was experiencing a great deal of stress over her son's divorce—Marian is still trying to forgive her daughter-in-law for running off with the sheriff's deputy—she found herself drawn to the crystal punch bowl a fourth time, after she was certain no one was watching. Marian enjoys a good reputation around town, and she wasn't going to let anyone ruin it by implying that Marian was tipsy. Poor old Sandy Mitchell still hasn't recovered from the rumor that her DAR membership papers had been falsified. Marian would bet her best pair of Ferragamo pumps that she knows who spread that little canard. She can't prove it, though, and Marian isn't one to run around dispensing unsubstantiated gossip.

So once Marian feels sure the coast is clear, she savors each slow sip of that last cup of Virginia's secret recipe rum punch. Marian does feel a little tingly, she must admit, but she still has complete control of her faculties. Driving home, she is extra careful to come to a complete halt at each stop sign, and she keeps her hands planted firmly at ten and two.

Quite frankly, Marian suspects that she ingested less of the punch than most of the women. When she gathered her purse and said her good-byes, she would swear (if she were the kind of woman who swore), that Lydia Foxton was listing to the left a little in front of the antique sideboard in the living room.

In reality, none of the women need have worried about their ability to navigate the streets of Luckettville, for there isn't any rum in Virginia's secret recipe rum punch, nary a drop. It is a little inside joke, one the Tarver family has been passing down for generations.

Marian is making her careful way home as Virginia clears the dining room table from the ladies' most recent gathering. *No harm done,* Virginia thinks to herself. *The women enjoyed themselves, I got to show off my culinary skills, and summer is now officially in full swing.* Virginia puts the dessert plates in hot soapy water to soak before pulling out the bottle of Mogen David from under the kitchen sink and pouring a small glass to toast herself on a job well done.

BROILED GRAPEFRUIT

Brown sugar brings out the tartness in grapefruit. This is a great brunch or breakfast treat.

3 large grapefruits, peeled and sliced into rounds
1/3 cup brown sugar
2 tablespoons butter, diced
1/2 teaspoon cinnamon

Preheat the oven to 500 degrees. Lightly grease a 13 x 9-inch baking pan.

Cut each grapefruit into 4 slices. Place the slices in the baking pan. Sprinkle with the brown sugar. Dot each slice with butter and sprinkle with cinnamon. Broil the grapefruit until the juice is bubbling and the sugar begins to brown, about 1 to 2 minutes. Remove to a serving dish and drizzle with the pan juices. Serve hot.

Makes 6 servings

WHITE SULPHUR SPRINGS APPLE SORBET

This is a variation of a recipe I learned to make at the Greenbrier in West Virginia, my favorite vacation spot in the whole world.

12 cups apple juice
1/2 cup lemon juice
1 1/2 cups sugar

Mix the apple juice, lemon juice, and sugar in a large saucepan. Bring to a boil and boil for 3 minutes. Cool completely in the refrigerator. Freeze in an ice cream maker, according to the manufacturer's directions.

Makes 10 to 12 servings

FRUIT SALSA WITH CINNAMON CHIPS

This is a great dish to serve at showers and parties. It's a sweet variation on the tomato-based salsas that we all love in the South.

Salsa
2 large kiwis, peeled and finely diced
2 large apples, peeled, cored, and finely diced (I use Fuji or Gala.)
2 cups raspberries, finely diced
1 pound fresh strawberries, finely diced
1/4 cup sugar or sugar substitute
2 tablespoons brown sugar
1/4 cup apricot preserves

Cinnamon Chips
1 package (8-inch) flour tortillas, 10 per package
Butter-flavored cooking spray
1 cup sugar
1 tablespoon cinnamon

To make the salsa: In a large bowl, thoroughly mix the kiwis, apples, raspberries, strawberries, sugar, brown sugar, and apricot preserves. Cover and refrigerate for 20 minutes.

To make the chips: Preheat the oven to 350 degrees. Lightly grease a 16 x 14-inch cookie sheet.

Lightly spray one side of each tortilla with butter-flavored spray. Cut into wedges and arrange in a single layer on the prepared pan. Combine the sugar and cinnamon in a small bowl. Sprinkle the wedges with the sugar mixture. Spray again with cooking spray. Bake 8 to 10 minutes. Cool and serve with the fruit salsa.

Makes 16 to 20 servings

WHITE AND DARK CHOCOLATE MOUSSE

At Christmas I like to serve this with lady fingers and garnished with crushed peppermint candy.

White Chocolate Mousse
1 (11-ounce) bag white chocolate chips
4 tablespoons water
2 cups heavy whipping cream

Dark Chocolate Mousse
3 ounces unsweetened chocolate, chopped into small pieces
2 cups heavy whippping cream
3/4 cup sugar

To make the white chocolate mousse: Fill the bottom of a double boiler with 2 inches of water. Place the chocolate chips and water in the top of the double boiler. Place over medium heat and stir constantly until the chocolate and water are melted together, 2 to 3 minutes. Remove from over the water and keep at room temperature.

Whip the cream in the bowl of an electric mixer. Beat at high speed until the cream is stiff. Using a whisk, vigorously whip 1/3 of the cream into the melted white chocolate. Fold the chocolate mixture into the remaining whipped cream until smooth. Refrigerate 3 hours before serving.

To make the dark chocolate mousse: Place the chopped chocolate in the top of a double boiler over medium heat. Tightly cover with plastic wrap and allow to heat for 3 to 5 minutes. Remove from the heat and stir until smooth. Let cool to room temperature.

Whip together the heavy cream and sugar in the bowl of an electric mixer on medium speed for 5 minutes, until soft peaks form. Using a whisk, vigorously whip 1 1/2 cups of the cream into the cooled chocolate. Add the chocolate mixture to the remaining whipped cream, and use a rubber spatula to fold together until smooth. Refrigerate 3 hours before serving.

To serve: Alternate the white and dark chocolate in a serving dish or meringue shells. Garnish with fresh raspberries or layer with lady fingers, and top with whipped cream. At Christmastime garnish with crushed peppermint candy.

Makes 10 to 12 servings

Pear Pie with Cheddar Cheese Pastry

I love the combination of pears and cheddar cheese.

Pastry
2 cups all-purpose flour
$3/4$ cup sharp cheddar cheese, grated
$1/2$ teaspoon salt
$2/3$ cup cold butter, sliced into tablespoons
5 tablespoons ice water, divided

Filling
5 to 7 firm ripe pears, peeled and
     sliced (5 cups)
2 tablespoons lemon juice
$2/3$ cup sugar

$1/4$ cup all-purpose flour
$1/4$ teaspoon salt
$1/2$ teaspoon cinnamon
1 tablespoon honey
2 tablespoons butter

Topping
1 cup reserved pastry mixture
$1/2$ cup brown sugar
1 teaspoon cinnamon
$1/4$ teaspoon ground cloves

To make the pastry: In a large bowl, mix the flour, cheese, and salt together. Mix the butter in with your fingers until the mixture is crumbly. Remove 1 cup of the crumb mixture and set aside for the topping. Stir in the ice water, one tablespoon at a time, until the mixture forms a dough. Wrap and chill in the refrigerator for 30 minutes. When completely chilled, roll the dough to fit a 10-inch pie plate.

To make the filling: Preheat the oven to 350 degrees. Place the pears in a large bowl and sprinkle with lemon juice. Add the sugar, flour, salt, cinnamon, and honey. Toss to combine, and pour the pears into the pie crust. Dot with the butter and sprinkle with the topping.

To make the topping: In a small bowl, mix the reserved pastry mixture with brown sugar, cinnamon, and cloves. Sprinkle over the pear filling. Bake 1 hour. Cool slightly before serving.

Makes 8 servings

STRAWBERRY ICE CREAM PIE

Any frozen dessert will cut easier if you run hot water over your knife before you use it.

1 cup chocolate wafer crumbs
$1/4$ cup butter, softened
$1/2$ cup pecans, finely chopped
1 (1.5 quart) container vanilla ice cream, softened
1 (15-ounce) container frozen strawberries, slightly thawed
$1/2$ cup chocolate sauce for topping

Preheat the oven to 350 degrees. Mix the chocolate crumbs, butter, and pecans in a 9-inch pie pan. Press into the pan, covering the bottom and sides. Bake 6 minutes. Cool.

Spoon $1/2$ of the vanilla ice cream over the cooled crust, then $1/2$ of the strawberries. Repeat; finishing with the strawberries. Garnish with chocolate sauce. Freeze overnight. Let sit 10 minutes before serving.

Makes 6 to 8 servings

VANILLA SOUFFLÉ WITH CHOCOLATE SAUCE

Put this in the oven exactly half an hour before you want to serve dessert. If you like to eat dessert right after the main course, put it in the oven just as you are serving dinner.

Soufflé

3 tablespoons butter, plus more for buttering soufflé dish

1 tablespoon plus $1/3$ cup sugar, divided

3 tablespoons all-purpose flour

1 cup milk

5 egg yolks, beaten

2 teaspoons vanilla extract

7 large egg whites

$1/2$ teaspoon cream of tartar

Chocolate Sauce

$1/3$ cup cocoa

1 cup sugar

1 cup light corn syrup

$1/2$ cup light whipping cream

3 tablespoons butter

1 teaspoon vanilla extract

To make the soufflé: Preheat the oven to 375 degrees. Butter a 6-cup soufflé dish, and sprinkle with 1 tablespoon sugar. Melt the 3 tablespoons butter in a small saucepan over low heat. Add the flour and stir with a wooden spoon to mix well. Remove from the heat, and add $1/3$ cup sugar and the milk. Return to the heat and whisk quickly until the mixture comes to a boil and is smooth. Whisk in the beaten egg yolks and vanilla.

In the bowl of an electric mixer, beat the egg whites with the cream of tartar until stiff. Gently fold into the yolk mixture. Pour into the prepared soufflé dish and bake for 30 minutes. When ready to serve, bring to the table hot. Use 2 forks held back to back to make an opening in the center and add $1/4$ cup chocolate sauce. Spoon the soufflé onto serving dishes, and spoon the remaining sauce over each serving.

To make the chocolate sauce: Mix the cocoa and sugar together in a small saucepan. Add the corn syrup, cream, and butter. Place over medium heat. Stir with a wooden spoon until the mixture boils. Boil 3 minutes, stirring constantly. Add vanilla.

Makes 4 to 6 servings

WHITE CHOCOLATE SOUP WITH BROWNIES

A restaurant close to my son's home serves a variation on this dessert. When he gets to pick the restaurant, that is usually the one he chooses, just for this dessert.

White Chocolate Soup
1 cup white chocolate chips
1 (13.5-ounce) can coconut milk
1 cup heavy whipping cream
1/8 teaspoon salt
1/2 teaspoon vanilla extract
Raspberries, for garnish

Brownies
1/2 cup butter
1 cup sugar
1/4 cup cocoa
2 large eggs, slightly beaten
3/4 cup all-purpose flour
1/2 cup pecans, optional
1 teaspoon vanilla extract

To make the soup: Place the white chocolate chips in a medium heat-resistant bowl. Heat the coconut milk, heavy cream, and salt together in a medium saucepan. Bring to a boil, and boil for 2 minutes. Add the vanilla extract, and then pour the mixture over the chocolate chips. Cover with plastic wrap. Stir after 5 minutes. This soup can be prepared ahead of time and reheated for serving.

To make the brownies: Preheat the oven to 300 degrees. Grease and flour a 9-inch square baking pan.

In a medium saucepan, melt together the butter, sugar, and cocoa over low heat. Add the eggs, flour, pecans, and vanilla. Stir to combine. Bake 30 minutes. Let cool slightly. Cut into squares. Place a square in the bottom of a soup bowl. Pour hot soup over the brownie and garnish with raspberries.

Makes 6 servings

WHITE CHOCOLATE PARTY MIX

This is downright addictive.

1 pound white chocolate
6 ounces Crispix cereal
5 ounces pretzel rounds
1 1/2 cups salted peanuts
8 ounces chocolate-coated candies
1/2 cup pecans
1/2 cup raisins

Melt the white chocolate in a double boiler over simmering water. Mix the Crispix cereal, pretzels, peanuts, chocolate-coated candies, pecans, and raisins in a large bowl. Pour the melted chocolate over the ingredients and mix carefully with a rubber spatula. Spread on waxed paper. When cooled and firm, break into small pieces. Store in an airtight container.

Makes 12 to 16 servings

NO RUM PUNCH

1 (46-ounce) can pineapple juice
1 tablespoon rum extract
1 pint orange sherbet, softened
1 quart vanilla ice cream, softened
1 liter ginger ale, chilled

In a large mixing bowl, place the pineapple juice, rum extract, orange sherbet, and vanilla ice cream. Stir until blended. Pour into a punch bowl, and gently stir in the ginger ale.

Makes 18 to 24 servings

Strawberries on a Cloud

This light dessert is great to serve after a heavy meal or at any ladies lunch.

4 large egg whites
$1/4$ teaspoon salt
$1/4$ teaspoon cream of tartar
1 cup sugar
4 teaspoons cornstarch
2 teaspoons vanilla extract
1 cup heavy whipping cream
2 tablespoons powdered sugar
4 cups strawberries, sliced

Preheat the oven to 275 degrees. Lightly butter and flour a large cookie sheet.

Beat the egg whites, salt, and cream of tartar in the bowl of an electric mixer at high speed until stiff peaks form. Gradually add the sugar, beating until the mixture is glossy. Beat in the cornstarch and vanilla. Using a large spoon, place 8 mounds of the egg whites on the baking sheet, 2 inches apart. Use the back of the spoon to smooth and make a small indentation, like a nest in the middle of each mound. Bake 1 $1/2$ hours or until the meringue shells feel dry to the touch. Cool.

In the bowl of an electric mixer, add the whipping cream and powdered sugar, and beat on high until soft peaks form. Place in the refrigerator until ready to use.

To serve, fill each nest with sliced strawberries. Top with the whipped cream, and serve immediately.

Makes 8 servings

Pecan Cobbler

There is nothing better than this cobbler with vanilla ice cream on top.

1 cup sugar
$1/2$ cup brown sugar
1 cup light corn syrup
$1/3$ cup butter, melted
$1/4$ teaspoon salt
2 teaspoons vanilla extract
6 large eggs, slightly beaten
3 cups pecans, coarsely chopped
Pie crust (see recipe on page 37 for Peach Cobbler)

Preheat the oven to 350 degrees. Lightly grease a 13 x 9-inch baking pan.

In a large bowl, combine the sugar, brown sugar, corn syrup, butter, salt, and vanilla. Whisk and beat in the eggs. Spread $1/3$ of the mixture over the bottom of the prepared pan. Stir the chopped pecans into the remaining mixture and set aside. Roll out the pie crust dough into a 13 x 9-inch rectangle, and place it on top of the filling. Spread the remaining mixture on top of the crust. Bake 40 minutes, or until the center is almost set. Serve warm or at room temperature.

Makes 10 to 12 servings

PECAN COOKIE CUPS

Fill with your favorite ice cream or fresh fruit. You can also fill these with mousse or pudding.

1/3 cup brown sugar, firmly packed
1/4 cup butter
1/4 cup light corn syrup
1/3 cup all-purpose flour
1/2 cup pecans, finely chopped
1/2 teaspoon vanilla extract

Preheat the oven to 350 degrees. Cover a large cookie sheet with parchment paper. Top the parchment paper with four 6-inch squares of additional parchment paper.

Combine the brown sugar, butter, and corn syrup in a small saucepan. Cook over low heat until the butter melts and the sugar is dissolved, stirring constantly. Remove from the heat, and stir in the flour, pecans, and vanilla. Drop 1 tablespoon of batter on each of the four squares of paper. Bake 10 minutes or until golden brown. Lift each paper, one at a time, and allow the cookie to rest on a solid surface for 10 seconds. Turn each cookie upside down over a small bowl or cup to form a crisp shell. If the cookie becomes too hard for this process, return it to the oven for a few seconds. Repeat the process until all the cookie batter is used. The cookies will be very crisp. Store in an airtight container. This can be done 1 week ahead.

Makes 10 servings

Molten Chocolate Cakes

My beautiful granddaughter, Paige, learned to make this when she was fourteen years old.
She is already a wonderful hostess and serves this as her signature dessert.

4 (1-ounce) squares semi-sweet baking chocolate
1/2 cup butter
1 cup powdered sugar
2 large eggs
2 large egg yolks
6 tablespoons all-purpose flour
Whipped topping or vanilla ice cream

Preheat the oven to 425 degrees. Butter four 3/4-cup custard cups or soufflé dishes. Place on a baking sheet.

Microwave the chocolate and butter in a large microwaveable bowl on high heat for 1 minute or until the butter is melted. Stir with a whisk until the chocolate is completely melted. Stir in the sugar until well blended. Whisk in the eggs and egg yolks. Stir in the flour. Divide the batter between the prepared custard cups. Bake 13 to 14 minutes or until the sides are firm, but the centers are soft. Let stand 1 minute. Carefully run a small knife around the edges to loosen the cakes. Invert cakes onto dessert dishes. Serve immediately, topped with whipped topping or ice cream.

Makes 4 servings

FROZEN STRAWBERRY SALAD

This Southern dish has been around for decades because it is absolutely delicious. It is a staple at ladies lunches.

4 ounces cream cheese, softened
$1/2$ cup mayonnaise
$1/4$ cup pineapple juice (from the crushed pineapple)
1 (8-ounce) container frozen whipped topping, thawed
1 (24-ounce) package frozen sliced strawberries, thawed
2 medium bananas, diced
1 (20-ounce) can crushed pineapple, drained, $1/4$ cup liquid reserved

Place the cream cheese in a large mixing bowl. Add the mayonnaise and pineapple juice. Mix well. Fold in the whipped topping. Add the strawberries, bananas, and pineapple. Mix well. Pour into a 13 x 9-inch glass dish or a mold of your choice. Cover and freeze overnight.

Makes 16 servings

NO-CRUST FUDGE PIE

Sometimes you just don't have time to make a pie crust or may not have one in the freezer. This is delicious, quick, and easy. And it sure does taste good with peppermint ice cream on top.

1 cup sugar
2 large eggs, slightly beaten
1 (1-ounce) square unsweetened chocolate, or $1/3$ cup cocoa
$1/2$ cup butter
$1/2$ cup all-purpose flour
$1/4$ teaspoon salt
1 teaspoon vanilla extract
$1/2$ cup pecans, chopped

Preheat the oven to 350 degrees. Grease a 9-inch pie pan.

Beat the sugar and eggs together in a medium mixing bowl. In a small saucepan over low heat, melt the chocolate and butter together. Add to the egg mixture. Stir in the flour, salt, and vanilla. Sprinkle the top with the chopped pecans. Bake 25 to 30 minutes.

Makes 6 to 8 servings

LEMON-FILLED CAKE ROLL

This is one of the prettiest desserts I make.

Cake
4 large eggs, separated
3/4 cup sugar, divided
1 teaspoon lemon extract
1 tablespoon vegetable oil
2/3 cup cake flour
1 teaspoon baking powder
1/4 teaspoon salt
1/4 cup powdered sugar

Lemon Filling
1 (14-ounce) can condensed milk
1/3 cup lemon juice
4 drops yellow food coloring
1 cup frozen non-dairy whipped topping,
   thawed

Coconut Topping
1 cup flaked coconut
1 teaspoon water
3 drops yellow food coloring

To make the cake: Preheat the oven to 375 degrees. Grease a 15 x 10 x 1-inch baking pan. Line with parchment paper, and grease and flour the paper.

Beat the 4 egg whites in the bowl of an electric mixer until foamy, and gradually add 1/2 cup of sugar. Continue to beat until stiff and soft peaks form when the mixer beaters are lifted. Set aside. Beat the egg yolks until light and lemon colored, gradually adding the remaining 1/4 cup sugar, beating constantly. Stir in the lemon extract and oil. Sift together the cake flour, baking powder, and salt in a small bowl. Fold the egg yolk mixture into the beaten egg whites, mixing well. Fold in the flour mixture. Spread the batter evenly over the prepared pan. Bake 10 minutes. Sift 1/4 cup powdered sugar evenly over a large linen towel. When the cake is done, immediately loosen the cake from the sides of the pan and turn out onto the towel. Peel off the parchment paper. Starting at the narrow end, roll up the cake and towel together. Place seam side down on a wire rack to cool.

To make the filling: In a medium bowl, combine the milk, lemon juice, and food coloring, stirring to mix well. Fold in the whipped topping.

To make the topping: Combine the coconut, water, and food coloring in a small plastic bag. Shake the bag to color the coconut.

To assemble: Unroll the cake, and spread with half of the lemon filling. Reroll and place on a serving plate with the seam side down. Spread the remaining filling on the sides and ends. Sprinkle with the coconut. Refrigerate 2 hours before serving. To serve, slice into 1-inch slices.

Makes 10 servings

Chocolate Banana Caramel Cream Pie

Let me say right up front that this pie is a lot of work, but it sure is worth the effort.

Caramel Filling
1 (14-ounce) can sweetened condensed milk

Chocolate Filling
1/2 cup semi-sweet chocolate chips
1/3 cup heavy whipping cream
1 tablespoon light corn syrup

1 (9-inch) pie crust, baked

Cream Filling
1/3 cup sugar
2 tablespoons cornstarch

1/8 teaspoon salt
1 1/2 cups light cream
2 large egg yolks, slightly beaten
1 teaspoon vanilla extract
2 tablespoons butter

2 large bananas, sliced

Topping
1 cup heavy cream, whipped
1/4 cup pecans, toasted and chopped

To make the caramel filling: Place the unopened can in a 2-quart saucepan. Cover with water. Bring to a simmer over low heat. Simmer for 3 hours. Keep the can covered at all times with water. Cool before using.

To make the chocolate filling: Place the semi-sweet chocolate chips in a medium bowl. Pour the heavy cream into a small saucepan and heat over medium until bubbles begin to form around the edges. Pour the hot milk over the chocolate. Slowly stir until the chocolate melts. Add the corn syrup, stir, and pour into the pie crust. Refrigerate until ready to assemble.

To make the cream filling: In a medium saucepan, whisk together the sugar, cornstarch, and salt. Whisk in the light cream and egg yolks. Place over medium heat. Bring to a boil, stirring constantly for about 4 minutes or until thickened. Remove from heat, and add vanilla and butter. Cool for 1 hour.

To assemble: Pour the caramel on top of the chocolate. Top with the sliced bananas. Spread the cooled cream filling over the bananas. Top with the whipped cream and toasted pecans.

Makes 8 servings

RED VELVET CHEESECAKE

This is perfect for any time of the year, but it's a must for Valentine's Day.

Crust
1 2/3 cups chocolate graham cracker crumbs
1/4 cup sugar
1/2 cup butter, melted

Filling
1 pound semi-sweet chocolate chips
1/2 cup butter, melted
4 (8-ounce) packages cream cheese, softened
1 cup sour cream

1/2 cup sugar
1/3 cup buttermilk
1 (1-ounce) bottle red food coloring
    (2 tablespoons)
5 large eggs

Topping
1 1/2 cups sour cream
1/4 cup sugar
1/2 teaspoon vanilla extract

To make the cheesecake: Preheat the oven to 350 degrees. Lightly grease a 10 x 3-inch springform pan.

Mix the chocolate crumbs, sugar, and butter together in a small bowl. Press into the bottom and 2 inches up the side of the springform pan. Bake 5 minutes. Let cool while you make the filling. Do not turn off the oven.

To make the filling: Combine the chocolate chips and butter in a medium saucepan over low heat, stirring until melted. Set aside to cool.

Combine the cooled chocolate mixture, cream cheese, 1 cup sour cream, sugar, buttermilk, and food coloring in the bowl of an electric mixer. Beat at high speed until the filling is smooth. Reduce the mixer speed to low, and add the eggs one at a time, just until combined.

Pour into the cooled crust. Place the filled springform pan on a baking pan. Reduce the oven temperature to 300 degrees. Bake 1 hour and 20 minutes, or until the cake appears set when gently shaken.

To make the topping: Mix the sour cream, sugar, and vanilla together in a small bowl. Spread over the cheesecake. Return to the oven, and cook for 5 minutes. Cool and chill for 6 hours or overnight before serving.

Makes 16 servings

No Flames, No Fuss Easy Bananas Foster

When you are in a restaurant, I highly recommend you order Bananas Foster with all the theatrics involved. I don't know about you, but I am not a big fan of setting things on fire in my home. This recipe is a great alternative to the traditional dessert without all of the drama.

1/4 cup butter
2 large bananas, sliced
1 cup light brown sugar
1 teaspoon vanilla extract
1/2 teaspoon cinnamon
1/4 teaspoon salt
4 scoops vanilla or praline-flavored ice cream

Melt the butter in a 9-inch iron skillet. Add the bananas and cook for 1 minute, stirring constantly. Add the brown sugar, vanilla, cinnamon, and salt, and continue to cook for 2 minutes, stirring constantly. Serve hot over ice cream.

Makes 2 servings

Chapter 4

REVEREND BOYDSTON COMES TO TOWN

When word came to Luckettville that All Souls Chapel was getting a new preacher, Lindsay Lancaster could hardly contain herself. It had been almost a year since Brother Steve had left, and they'd been stuck with one substitute after another while the bishop took his sweet time finding a permanent replacement. Lindsay just hoped the wait would be worth it. She had to admit they would be hard-pressed to find a finer man of the cloth than Brother Steve, but even he couldn't defy the hands of time. The entire church had realized he needed to hang up his robe after he forgot to dismiss the congregants one Sunday, causing them to remain seated in their pews until well past one waiting for the benediction, resulting in a rush to get in line at the Liberty Cafeteria before the prime rib ran out.

So while the faithful pilgrims of All Souls were delighted to hear that they would soon have a new leader, the chosen one, the Rev. Daniel Boydston, wasn't so sure. In fact, when Bishop Lawrence let Daniel know he was being assigned to a chapel in a town of some three thousand people—Daniel preferred the city—his first response was one of incredulity.

"There will be no debate," the bishop had said. "You need the experience of pastoring a small church if you are to continue serving the Lord."

Daniel, more than anything, wanted to serve the Lord. So it was with a sense of resignation, and a call to duty, that he'd loaded a rental truck and made the drive across the state to his new home. He had never had complete responsibility for a church before, having served only as an assistant pastor and youth director. Now his time had come.

Being told where to live was one part of his job description that Daniel didn't much care for, but there was a lot that Daniel did like about his job. The people, for one thing. Daniel thrived on being with believers of all ages as they made their way through the joys, and the tragedies, of life. Weddings, baptisms, divorces, graduations, funerals. He loved them all. Couples counseling, Vacation Bible School, even stewardship campaigns. Daniel could not get enough of the church.

Since moving back to Luckettville after college, about five years ago, Lindsay had jumped right into the happenings of All Souls Chapel. It's the church she was baptized and confirmed in, and she hoped to be married there one day. Serving as head of the All Souls' Hospitality Committee—she was also a member of the altar guild—was just one of the ways she stayed involved. So it fell to her to greet the new preacher on behalf of the faithful.

"We're having a welcome tea for you on Sunday," said Lindsay as she approached the preacher, soon after he pulled his car into the church parking lot for the first time.

"After the eleven o'clock, in the courtyard," she added, tucking in her blouse. She was trying not to flirt. Why hadn't anyone told her how handsome he was?

"Pray for sunshine."

Daniel was touched, of course, and a little nervous. If the rest of the congregation looked like Lindsay, he might have a hard time concentrating on the Good Book.

"I'll put in a word for us with the man upstairs," said Daniel, hoping he didn't sound as lame as he felt. "I've got connections."

Behind the scenes, the hospitality committee had been working for weeks to get things just right for the Rev. Daniel Boydston, who was rumored not to be bringing a wife or children with him. It had been awhile since All Souls had enjoyed a single pastor, as usually they drew the elderly clergy pulled out of retirement to help the church struggle through one more year. Now, though, with more and more families moving into the county, it seemed their luck might be changing.

As soon as the bishop let All Souls know his decision, the best cooks in the congregation had been tapped to work their culinary magic in honor of the Reverend Boydston's arrival. Anna Rae would bring her chocolate chip meringue bites, so light you could hold three in your hand at one time and still have room for some sugared nuts. Mrs. Dalton was making caramel candy, which was always a hit with young and old alike. You could count on Yancey Douglas, the only man on the hospitality committee, to provide cherry-apple fried pies. He prided himself on having perfected the art of the doughy delight, and he welcomed any excuse to drag out his mother's cast-iron skillet, seasoned just so. Even Lindsay, who didn't usually care for cherries,

had to admit they were delicious, not too tart. Her own offering would be a flourless chocolate cake, which she had learned to make back when she thought Mack Hutcheson was going to ask her to marry him. Lindsay had hoped her prowess in the kitchen would seal the deal, but even butter and sugar could not win Mack's heart, especially when his high school girlfriend scurried back to Luckettville after a disastrous try at pharmaceutical sales over in Baton Rouge. Susie McKenzie would bring toasted angel food cake with orange sauce, and no doubt refer to her cleverness in having thought to bring angel food cake to church. She would also be bringing her sister, the spinster.

As it turns out, Susie wasn't the only member of All Souls Chapel to consider the Rev. Daniel Boydston ripe for the picking, as it is standing room only that first Sunday, a crowd the likes of which the church hasn't seen in years.

"Why are so many women here?" Yancey Douglas whispers to his wife, who is too busy powdering her nose to respond. She wishes she had invited that sweet neighbor to come with them, the single gal with all the cats.

As for the Reverend Boydston, he hasn't seen so many good-looking women since his college days. When he steps into the pulpit, he notices Lindsay sitting on the front pew. Thankful for God's handiwork in all its various manifestations, it is all he can do not to wink at her. *Maybe this assignment won't be so bad after all*, thinks Daniel as he invites the congregation to join him in prayer.

HOMEMADE CARAMEL CANDY

This is sure to impress company.

4 cups sugar, divided
1 cup milk
$1/2$ teaspoon salt
2 cups pecans or walnuts (optional)
2 tablespoons butter

Lightly butter a 9-inch square dish. Place 1 cup of sugar in a 9-inch iron skillet over medium heat to caramelize. Stir as the sugar begins to turn brown. At the same time over medium heat, add the remaining sugar and the milk to a large saucepan. Stir occasionally while the sugar in the iron skillet is caramelizing. Once the sugar is brown, pour it into the milk mixture, stirring constantly. Cook to a soft ball stage (238 degrees). Remove from the heat and add the salt, nuts, and butter. Let cool for 5 minutes. Beat with a wooden spoon until creamy. This takes 5 to 8 minutes. Pour into the buttered dish. When cool, cut the candy into squares.

Makes 24 servings

SPONGE CAKE DELIGHT

My daughter, Kelly, makes this dessert all the time, and it is a big hit at her dinners and parties.

1 (1-pound) box cream-filled sponge cakes (10 individually wrapped)
1 (20-ounce) can crushed pineapple, drained
6 large bananas
2 (6-ounce) boxes French vanilla instant pudding mix
3 cups milk
1 (12-ounce) container frozen whipped topping, thawed
1 cup pecans, chopped

Slice the cream-filled sponge cakes lengthwise, and place in a 13 x 9-inch cake pan, filling side up. Pour the drained pineapple over the cakes. Slice the bananas lengthwise and lay on top of the pineapple. In a separate bowl, whisk together the pudding mix and milk according to directions. Pour the vanilla pudding over the bananas. Spread the whipped topping over the bananas, and sprinkle with the pecans. Place in the refrigerator 30 minutes before serving.

Makes 12 servings

WHITE CHOCOLATE BROWNIE CHEESECAKE

This decadent treat is a favorite of my cooking students.

Crust

1 1/2 cups graham cracker crumbs
2 tablespoons sugar
1/3 cup butter, melted

Cake

1 (11-ounce) package white chocolate chips
4 (8-ounce) packages cream cheese, softened
1/2 cup butter, softened
2/3 cup sugar
3 tablespoons all-purpose flour

4 large eggs
2 teaspoons vanilla extract
1/8 teaspoon salt
2 cups coarsely chopped brownies (see recipe on page 59 for Brownies)

Sour Cream Topping

1 1/2 cups sour cream
2/3 cup sugar
1 teaspoon vanilla extract

To make the crust: Lightly grease a 10-inch springform pan. Mix the graham cracker crumbs, sugar, and butter together. Press into the bottom and 1/2 inch up the sides of the springform pan. Chill for 1 hour.

To make the cake: Preheat the oven to 300 degrees. Place the white chocolate chips in the top of a double boiler over simmering water until the chocolate melts. Set aside to cool. Beat the cream cheese and butter at medium speed with an electric mixer until light and fluffy, about 2 minutes. In a small bowl, combine the sugar and flour. Add to the cheese mixture, beating well. Add the eggs one at a time, beating well after each addition. Add the cooled chocolate, vanilla, and salt. Pour half of the mixture into the springform pan. Top with the chopped brownies, and pour the remaining mixture over the brownies. Bake 1 hour.

To make the sour cream topping: In a small bowl, combine the sour cream, sugar, and vanilla, stirring well. Remove the cheesecake from the oven and top with the sour cream topping. Return to the oven for 10 minutes. Cover and chill 8 hours before serving.

Makes 12 servings

ALEZE'S CHOCOLATE MERINGUE PIE

This is the first pie I ever remember making. I was sixteen, and my mother was having company for dinner. I called my cousin Aleze on our eight-party-line phone, and she walked me through this. So there might be some others out there who were listening in and have this recipe too.

Pie
1 cup sugar
2 tablespoons cornstarch
1 tablespoon all-purpose flour
1/4 teaspoon salt
1/4 cup cocoa
2 1/4 cups milk
3 large egg yolks, beaten (reserve the whites for the meringue)
1 tablespoon butter
1 teaspoon vanilla extract
1 (9-inch) pie shell, baked

Meringue
3 large egg whites
1/2 teaspoon cream of tartar
6 tablespoons sugar

To make the pie: In a large saucepan, combine the sugar, cornstarch, flour, salt, and cocoa, stirring well. Gradually add the milk. Place the saucepan over medium-high heat and bring to a boil. Remove the saucepan from the heat, and temper 1/4 cup of the mixture into the beaten egg yolks. Stir the egg mixture back into the saucepan. Return to the heat and continue to boil for 3 to 5 minutes, stirring constantly. Add the butter and vanilla. Pour the mixture into the pie shell, and top with meringue.

To make the meringue: Preheat the oven to 350 degrees. In a large bowl, beat the egg whites and cream of tartar with an electric mixer until soft peaks form. Gradually beat in the sugar until the egg whites stand in stiff peaks. Spread over the pie and bake for 8 to 10 minutes or until golden brown.

Makes 6 to 8 servings

PURPLE PLUM GOOD PECAN BREAD

This is a beautiful addition to any table. It is also sure to cheer up anyone to whom you take a loaf.

1/2 cup butter, softened
1 cup sugar
1/2 teaspoon vanilla extract
2 large eggs
1 1/2 cups all-purpose flour
1/2 teaspoon salt
1/2 teaspoon cream of tartar
1/4 teaspoon baking soda
1/3 cup sour cream
1 teaspoon grated lemon zest
1 cup purple plums, chopped into 1/2-inch pieces
1/2 cup pecans, chopped
Cream cheese, optional

Preheat the oven to 350 degrees. Grease and flour a 9 x 5-inch loaf pan.

In a large bowl, cream the butter, sugar, and vanilla together with an electric mixer, until fluffy. Add the eggs one at a time, beating well after each addition. In a medium bowl, sift together the flour, salt, cream of tartar, and baking soda. In a small bowl, combine the sour cream and lemon zest. Alternately add the flour mixture and sour cream mixture to the batter. Stir in the plums and pecans. Pour into the loaf pan.

Bake 50 to 55 minutes, or until a toothpick inserted in the center of the bread comes out clean. Cool slightly and remove from the pan. If desired, spread the slices with cream cheese.

Makes 10 to 12 servings

DOWNTOWN DATE NUT MACAROON PIE

This recipe was inspired by a pie I used to enjoy years ago from a long-gone beloved restaurant in downtown Nashville where my sister used to eat every Sunday after church.

1 cup white saltine cracker crumbs (18 to 20 crackers)
1/2 cup dates, chopped
1/2 cup maraschino cherries, chopped
1 cup sugar
3/4 cup pecans, chopped
3 large egg whites
1/4 teaspoon baking powder
1 teaspoon vanilla extract

Preheat the oven to 375 degrees. Grease a 9-inch pie pan.

In a large mixing bowl, mix together the cracker crumbs, dates, maraschino cherries, sugar, and pecans and set aside. In a medium bowl, beat the egg whites with an electric mixer on high speed until stiff. Add the baking powder and vanilla to the egg whites, continuing to beat until mixed. Fold the beaten egg whites into the cracker-fruit mixture. Pour into the prepared pan. Bake 20 to 25 minutes or until golden brown. Cool before serving.

Makes 6 to 8 servings

Ribbon Pie

There's no reason you can't change the flavor of pudding in this pie to mix things up.

Crust

1 cup self-rising flour
1/2 cup butter
1/2 cup pecans, finely chopped

Filling

1 (5.1-ounce) package chocolate instant pudding and pie filling mix
3 cups milk
1 (8-ounce) package cream cheese, softened
1 cup sugar
1 (12-ounce) carton frozen whipped topping, thawed
1/2 cup pecans, chopped

To make the crust: Preheat the oven to 350 degrees. Combine the flour, butter, and pecans into a crumbly mix. Press the mixture into a 9-inch pie pan. Bake 20 minutes. Cool completely while making the filling.

To make the filling: In a medium bowl, mix the instant pudding with the milk. Whisk for 2 minutes. Refrigerate for 5 minutes. In a medium mixing bowl, cream together the cream cheese and sugar, using an electric mixer. Fold in the whipped topping.

To assemble: Spread half of the chocolate pudding into the crust. Then spread half of the cream cheese mixture. Repeat the layers, spreading to the edges. Sprinkle with the pecans. Refrigerate for 2 hours. Serve cold.

Makes 6 to 8 servings

SINFULLY DELICIOUS PECANS

I admire anyone who can eat only one-fourth cup of these.

2 large egg whites
1/2 teaspoon salt
1/2 teaspoon vanilla extract
1 pound brown sugar
1/2 teaspoon cayenne pepper
4 cups pecan halves
1/4 cup butter, melted and cooled

Preheat the oven to 300 degrees. Grease two 15 x 10-inch cookie sheets.

Using an electric mixer, beat the egg whites, salt, and vanilla together until stiff peaks form. Add the brown sugar and cayenne pepper, continuing to mix on medium speed for 3 minutes. Fold in the pecan halves and melted butter. Divide between the cookie sheets. Bake 20 to 25 minutes, stirring every 10 minutes. Pour out onto parchment paper, and separate with 2 forks to create individual sugar-coated pecans. Store in an airtight container for up to 2 weeks.

Makes 16 (1/4-cup) servings

CHERRY-APPLE FRIED PIES

This is a combination of two of my favorite fruits in one pie.

Crust

2 3/4 cup all-purpose flour
1 1/2 teaspoons salt
1 1/2 teaspoons sugar
1/2 cup vegetable shortening
1 medium egg, slightly beaten
2/3 cup evaporated milk

Filling

1 cup dried cherries
1 (5-ounce) package dried apples
1 tablespoon lemon juice
1 tablespoon butter
1/2 teaspoon cinnamon
1 cup sugar or sugar substitute

Flour for dusting the board
Oil for frying

To make the crust: In a large bowl, combine the flour, salt, sugar, and shortening. Using a pastry blender or your fingers, combine to form a crumbly mixture. Add the egg and evaporated milk, stirring until well mixed. Flatten the dough slightly, wrap in plastic wrap, and refrigerate for 30 minutes.

To make the filling: Place the cherries in a small saucepan over medium heat. Cover with water and bring to a boil. Reduce the heat to medium-low, and simmer for 30 minutes, stirring occasionally, and adding water as necessary. When the cherries are tender, continue to cook until the water has evaporated.

Place the apples in a medium saucepan and cover with water. Add the lemon juice. Bring to a boil. Reduce the heat to medium-low and simmer 1 hour. Add water as necessary, and stir occasionally. When the apples are tender, continue to cook until the water has evaporated. Add the butter, cinnamon, and sugar. Mash slightly with a potato masher. Stir in the cherries. Cool completely before making pies.

To assemble: Lightly flour a board, and roll the dough out to 1/4-inch thick. Cut into 5-inch circles. Place 1 1/2 tablespoons of filling in the center of each circle. Brush the edges with water, and fold over to seal. Prick the top with a fork. Add oil to an iron skillet so that it is 1/2-inch deep. When the oil is hot, fry the pies for 2 to 3 minutes per side. Drain on paper towels. Serve hot.

Makes 12 servings

Note: To test if the oil is hot enough, place a small piece of pie crust in the oil. When it begins to fry, remove it and begin frying the pies.

CHOCOLATE CHIP MERINGUE BITES

I used to cater a lot of local weddings and have been making these for more than forty years. They are still popular.

3 large egg whites
1/8 teaspoon salt
1/4 teaspoon cream of tartar
1 teaspoon vanilla extract
1 cup sugar
1 cup chocolate chips
1 cup pecans, chopped

Preheat the oven to 250 degrees. Lightly grease a large cookie sheet.

Place the egg whites in a large bowl. Add the salt, cream of tartar, and vanilla. Beat at high speed with an electric mixer until the egg whites stand in soft peaks. Slowly add the sugar. Fold in the chocolate chips and pecans with a rubber spatula. Drop by small spoonfuls onto the cookie sheet. Bake 1 hour or until dry to the touch.

Makes 48 servings

Variation: Omit the chocolate chips and pecans. Drop by small spoonfuls onto a cookie sheet. With the back of the spoon, make a small nest in each mound. Follow the baking instructions above. When ready to serve, put whipped cream in the center, topped with fresh fruit, such as strawberries, oranges, peaches, or raspberries.

Toasted Angel Food Cake with Orange Sauce

You can find angel food cake at any grocery store, but everyone should know how to make one. Especially if you find yourself with a large number of egg whites on hand. A big thank you to my sister Louise for this recipe. It has been a favorite of mine for years.

Cake

1 1/2 cups sugar, divided
1 cup sifted cake flour
1/2 teaspoon salt
1 1/4 cups large egg whites (10 to 12 eggs)
1 1/4 teaspoons cream of tartar
1 teaspoon vanilla extract
1/2 cup butter, melted

Orange Sauce

1/2 cup butter, softened
1 1/2 cups sugar
4 large egg yolks
1 tablespoon orange zest
2/3 cup orange juice
2/3 cup milk

To make the cake: Preheat the oven to 350 degrees. In a medium bowl, sift together 1/2 cup sugar and the cake flour twice and set aside. In the bowl of an electric mixer, add the salt, egg whites, and cream of tartar. Beat until soft peaks form. Add the remaining cup of sugar 1/4 cup at a time, beating after each addition. Fold in the vanilla and the sifted flour mixture.

Pour into an ungreased 10-inch tube pan. Bake 40 to 45 minutes. Invert on a cooling rack. Let cool prior to slicing.

To make the orange sauce: Mix the butter and sugar in the top of a double boiler. Stir well. Add the egg yolks, whisking after each addition. Add the orange zest, orange juice, and milk. Cook over simmering water for 10 to 15 minutes, stirring occasionally. Remove the double boiler from the heat and allow to cool.

To serve: Slice the cake into 1 1/2-inch thick slices. Brush both sides with the melted butter, and place under the broiler for 1 to 2 minutes or until golden brown. Serve with the orange sauce on top.

Makes 12 servings

DOUGHNUT BREAD PUDDING WITH VANILLA SAUCE

During development, this recipe was an overwhelming favorite among all of my recipe samplers.

Bread Pudding
12 regular doughnuts
1/2 cup raisins (optional)
1/2 cup butter, melted
1/2 cup sugar
5 large eggs
2 1/2 cups heavy whipping cream
1 teaspoon cinnamon
1 teaspoon vanilla extract

Vanilla Sauce
1/4 cup butter, melted
2 cups powdered sugar
1/4 cup evaporated milk
1/2 teaspoon cinnamon
1/2 teaspoon vanilla extract

To make the bread pudding: Preheat the oven to 350 degrees. Lightly butter a 13 x 9-inch baking pan.

Break the doughnuts into 1-inch pieces and layer them in the pan. Scatter the raisins over the doughnut pieces. Drizzle with the melted butter. In a medium bowl, whisk together the sugar, eggs, cream, cinnamon, and vanilla. Pour the cream mixture over the doughnuts. Let stand for 10 minutes. Cover with foil and bake for 30 minutes. Remove the foil and let brown for 10 minutes. Serve with the vanilla sauce.

To make the vanilla sauce: Whisk together the butter, powdered sugar, evaporated milk, cinnamon, and vanilla. Pour over the bread pudding.

Makes 12 servings

STRawbeRRy SNOWball cake

This is very popular at ladies events all over the South.

1 (6-ounce) package strawberry Jell-O
2 cups boiling water
1 cup sugar
3 tablespoons lemon juice
2 (10-ounce) packages frozen strawberries, thawed
2 (8-ounce) containers frozen whipped topping, thawed and divided
1 prepared angel food cake, broken into small pieces (8 cups)
Fresh strawberries, for garnish

Pour the boiling water into a large bowl. Stir the Jell-O into the boiling water to dissolve. Add the sugar and lemon juice, stirring until the sugar is dissolved. Refrigerate for 1 hour or until the Jell-O begins to thicken. Add the strawberries and 1 container of whipped topping. Fold in the cake pieces.

Pour the mixture into a 13 x 9-inch glass dish. Top with the additional whipped topping. Garnish with the fresh strawberries. Cover and refrigerate overnight.

Makes 12 servings

GRaPe ice CReaM

This will remind you of eating grape popsicles when you were a child.

2 cups sugar
1 (12-ounce) can frozen grape juice, thawed
4 cups water
$1/2$ cup lemon juice
2 cups light whipping cream
2 cups heavy whipping cream
1 (12-ounce) can evaporated milk

In a large bowl, add the sugar, grape juice, and water. Stir until the sugar is dissolved. Add the lemon juice. In a second large bowl, combine the creams and evaporated milk. Add the cream mixture to the grape juice mixture. Pour into a 1-gallon ice cream freezer. Freeze according to the manufacturer's directions.

Makes 12 servings

CHERRY MUFFINS WITH WHITE CHOCOLATE CHIPS

These are a big hit in my Sunday school class.

Muffins

1/2 cup butter, softened

1 cup sugar

2 large eggs

1 teaspoon vanilla extract

2 cups all-purpose flour

3 teaspoons baking powder

1/2 teaspoon salt

1 cup sour cream

1 pound frozen dark sweet cherries, rinsed, thawed, and chopped

1 cup white chocolate chips

Topping

1/3 cup brown sugar

1/2 cup pecans, finely chopped

1/2 teaspoon cinnamon

To make the muffins: Preheat the oven to 375 degrees. Grease 2 (12-cup) muffin tins or use paper liners.

In a medium mixing bowl, beat the butter and sugar until creamy. Beat in the eggs one at a time until fluffy. Add the vanilla. In a medium bowl, combine the flour, baking powder, and salt. Alternately add the flour mixture and the sour cream to the batter and beat until completely mixed. Fold in the chopped cherries and the chocolate chips, stirring only to combine. Fill the muffin tins 2/3 full.

To make the topping: In a small bowl, combine the brown sugar, pecans, and cinnamon. Sprinkle the brown sugar mixture over the batter.

Bake 25 minutes or until golden brown. Cool for 10 minutes before removing from the pan.

Makes 24 servings

FLOURLESS CHOCOLATE CAKE

If cake making isn't your finest skill, try this one. It is easy and delicious.

Cake
Cocoa powder for dusting
1 cup semi-sweet chocolate chips
1/2 cup butter
3/4 cup sugar
3 large eggs, beaten
1/4 teaspoon salt
1 teaspoon vanilla extract

Ganache
1/2 cup heavy whipping cream
1 cup chocolate chips
1/2 teaspoon vanilla extract
Raspberries for garnish (optional)

To make the cake: Preheat the oven to 300 degrees. Grease an 8-inch round cake pan with butter and sprinkle with cocoa powder.

Melt the chocolate chips and butter in the top of a double boiler, over simmering water, stirring until melted. Remove from the heat. Stir in the sugar, eggs, salt, and vanilla. Pour into the prepared cake pan. Bake 30 to 35 minutes or until a toothpick inserted in the middle of the cake comes out clean. Cool slightly in the pan. Turn onto a serving plate and spread with chocolate ganache.

To make the ganache: In a small saucepan, bring the cream to a boil. Place the chocolate chips in a medium bowl, and pour the warmed cream over the chocolate chips, stirring often until smooth. Add the vanilla. Cool slightly. Pour over the cake.

Garnish with raspberries if desired.

Makes 8 servings

Chapter 5

❧ ⋯✦⋯ ❧

AUNT CARLISLE CUTS BACK—A LITTLE

Having celebrated her eighty-sixth birthday recently, Aunt Carlisle is determined to make it to ninety, in part to spite those family members who had written her off years ago, predicting she'd croak the minute her husband passed.

"She won't last a week without Uncle Hank," whispered her great-nephew.

"The woman's never worked a day in her life," responded her second double cousin. "How in the world will she survive?"

Carlisle knows full well she isn't the first woman in the history of Clarke County to be underestimated, but still she resented it, especially when her relatives had the gall to make such comments in her own dining room, in between bites of stuffed eggs and ham biscuits after Hank's funeral. Who did they think took care of the house and the children while Hank was working down at the courthouse?

Hank had been a lovely man, a good provider, and a faithful husband. He'd always cleaned his plate, rarely sworn, and often surprised Carlisle with a bouquet of Queen Anne's lace, her favorite, for no reason. But Hank had never so much as changed a diaper or called a repairman in all their time together. Carlisle had done those things, so she felt sure she could figure out how to make it on her own until she was called up to the pearly gates herself. In fact, Carlisle is full of joy and thanksgiving that the good Lord has seen fit to keep her above ground for more than a decade since Hank had died, even though she misses him terribly, of course.

Carlisle has the same complaints as most folks her age, a little arthritis in her knees and a tendency to nod off during lunch. If she were honest with herself, she'd have to admit that she doesn't always eat right and often forgets to take her vitamins. Recently, though, she's been making a concerted effort to eat more healthily, and every evening when the weather is good, she takes a walk around the neighborhood. Her granddaughter is scheduled to graduate from medical school in a few months, and Carlisle wants to wear her pale blue suit, the one with the short sleeves and the scalloped collar. The last time she wore that suit, it had been a little snug, and Carlisle is determined not to spend money on a new dress. Finch women were known for making do with what they had.

Carlisle does love to eat; she admits that. Having grown up in a house of wonderful cooks, it was nothing short of a miracle that Carlisle didn't weigh more than she did. She can practically taste her mother's blueberry cream pie just by thinking about it, not to mention her grandmother's apple cake, which came with a caramel glaze that melted in your mouth. Now Carlisle is the keeper of those treasured recipes, housed in a small, three-ring binder coming apart at the spine. Carlisle can't bring herself to replace it and, instead, has wrapped a big rubber band around the black book that holds generations of her family's handwriting. She wouldn't let go of that book for anything.

Carlisle learned her way around the kitchen when she was a teenager, and since then she's made a name for herself in town— Carlisle doesn't like to brag, but a fact is a fact—with the desserts she made for the annual Luckettville Chamber of Commerce bake sale. She suspects that some people tried to befriend her simply because of her way with food. There's really no other reason, not to Carlisle's mind anyway, why somebody like the standoffish Millie Haverton would have anything to do with Carlisle if she wasn't such a good cook.

Now that Carlisle is paying closer attention to her health, she has resolved to rework some of her favorite recipes, thinking there might be some substitutions she could try. Didn't she read something in the *Luckettville Gazette* about using apple juice concentrate instead of sugar in muffins? She will also drink eight glasses of water a day, walk for forty-five minutes in the evenings instead of thirty, and try not to eat after seven at night. That last one will be tough because Carlisle has gotten used to enjoying a little snack at night while watching *Antiques Road Show* and *Masterpiece Theatre*.

Carlisle knows herself well enough to know that she will have to do this the natural way. She doesn't want to end up like her cousin Jo Nell, who lost fifty pounds on a diet that involved daily shots of some mysterious hormone and copious amounts of wheatgrass. Jo Nell looked great for about six months before she regained every pound and then some. Come to think of it, Carlisle hasn't seen Jo Nell in ages.

"Remind me to call and check on her," Carlisle says to herself; the talking out loud is a habit she developed after Hank died.

Carlisle heads toward the grocery store, determined to experiment with her favorite dessert recipes so as to stay one step ahead of the Grim Reaper. Instead of parking near the door like she usually does, Carlisle chooses a spot near the edge of the lot so she can get some exercise. *See, this is working already*, she thinks to herself as she grabs a cart.

Carlisle will do what she can, of course, but she doubts she can give up her apple cake with caramel glaze or caramel popcorn with peanuts. Carlisle has a thing for caramel, it's true. Those treats are her all-time favorites, and she will do just about anything to continue enjoying those indulgences—on occasion.

She'll make it work somehow because Carlisle Finch is nothing if not determined, just as the generation that came before her.

Fresh Blueberry Cream Pie

I am so glad blueberries are good for you. They are one of my favorite fruits to cook with, and I enjoy them raw as well.

Filling
1 cup sour cream
2 tablespoons all-purpose flour
1 cup sugar
1 teaspoon vanilla extract
$1/8$ teaspoon salt
1 large egg, slightly beaten
2 cups fresh blueberries, rinsed and drained
1 (9-inch) pie crust, unbaked

Topping
$1/4$ cup all-purpose flour
$1/4$ cup butter, softened
$1/4$ cup pecans, chopped

To make the filling: Preheat the oven to 375 degrees. In a small mixing bowl, combine the sour cream, flour, sugar, vanilla, salt, and egg. Beat for 3 to 4 minutes. Fold in the blueberries. Spoon the mixture into the crust. Bake 30 minutes.

To make the topping: Combine the flour and butter until it forms a crumbly mixture. Add the pecans and mix well. Remove the pie from the oven and sprinkle the topping over the filling. Bake an additional 10 minutes or until golden brown.

Makes 6 to 8 servings

Sugar-Free Peach Ice Cream

This recipe was given to me by my friend Aline Lampley. While it is sugar-free, it is not calorie-free. You can make it a little lighter by using low-fat milk products.

4 cups peaches, peeled and chopped
1 1/2 cups sugar substitute
1 (12-ounce) can evaporated milk
1 (3-ounce) package sugar-free vanilla instant pudding mix
1 quart light whipping cream
2 cups heavy whipping cream
2 cups milk
2 teaspoons vanilla extract

Place the peaches in a large bowl. (If you like the pieces smaller, you can either mash them coarsely or blend them in the food processor.) Cover the peaches with the sugar substitute, and place in the refrigerator for 1 hour. In a large bowl, whisk together the evaporated milk, instant pudding mix, light and heavy creams, milk, and vanilla. Place in an ice cream freezer, along with the peaches, and freeze according to the manufacturer's directions.

Makes 1 gallon

CARAMEL POPCORN WITH PEANUTS

I remember my mother making this when I was a little girl. Of course, she didn't have a microwave. She popped the popcorn over the fireplace.

2 (2.9-ounce) packages microwave popcorn, popped
1 cup butter
1/2 cup light corn syrup
2 tablespoons molasses
2 cups firmly packed brown sugar
1 teaspoon baking soda
1 teaspoon vanilla extract
1 1/2 cups salted peanuts

Preheat the oven to 250 degrees. Lightly grease two 15 x 11-inch baking pans.

Place the popped corn in a large mixing bowl. Melt the butter in a medium saucepan over medium heat. Add the corn syrup, molasses, and brown sugar. Stir occasionally until the mixture begins to boil. Using a candy thermometer, cook to a soft ball stage (238 degrees). Remove from the heat, and add the baking soda and vanilla.

Pour over the popcorn, and use a spatula to fold in the mixture until the popcorn is completely coated. Fold in the peanuts. Divide between the prepared pans, and place in the oven for 15 minutes. When the popcorn is cool, break into small pieces and store in an airtight container for up to 2 weeks.

Makes 8 servings

CHERRY CHEESECAKE BARS

It's awfully hard when you have to give up sweets because your pants start getting a little tight. But using sugar substitutes will make it a bit easier.

$2/3$ cup all-purpose flour
$2/3$ cup quick-cooking oats
$1/4$ cup brown sugar substitute
$1/4$ cup pecans, finely chopped
$1/4$ cup butter
2 (8-ounce) packages cream cheese, softened
$1/2$ cup sugar substitute
2 teaspoons vanilla extract
4 large eggs, lightly beaten
$1/2$ cup dried cherries, finely chopped

Preheat the oven to 350 degrees. Grease an 8-inch square baking pan.

In a medium bowl, mix together the flour, oats, brown sugar, pecans, and butter until the mixture resembles coarse crumbs. Press the crumbs into the prepared pan, and bake for 12 to 15 minutes. While the crust is baking, mix together the cream cheese, sugar, and vanilla in a medium bowl, until light and fluffy. Gradually add the eggs, beating on low speed just until combined. Stir in the cherries. Spread over the partially baked crust.

Bake 20 to 25 minutes or until the cream cheese layer is set. Cool at least 2 hours before serving. Store leftovers in the refrigerator.

Makes 8 to 10 servings

GaY TaYLoR's RaiSiN BRaN MUFFiNS

My friend Gay Taylor takes these to work all the time, and her coworkers love them. If you have a lot of coworkers, you can double the ingredients and make a larger batch.

2 1/2 cups self-rising flour
1 cup sugar
1/4 teaspoon cinnamon
1/4 teaspoon allspice
1/4 cup brown sugar
2 1/2 teaspoons baking soda
7 1/2 ounces crunchy raisin bran cereal
1 cup pecans, chopped
2 cups buttermilk
1/2 cup vegetable oil
2 large eggs, beaten

Place the flour in a large mixing bowl. Add the sugar, cinnamon, allspice, brown sugar, baking soda, cereal, and pecans, stirring to mix well. In a medium bowl, mix together the buttermilk, oil, and eggs. Add to the cereal mixture, and mix well. Cover and place the muffin mix in the refrigerator overnight.

Preheat the oven to 400 degrees. Grease or line 30 muffin tins. Fill each cup 2/3 full. Bake 20 minutes.

Makes 30 muffins

Note: This batter will keep in the refrigerator for up to 2 weeks.

peach sorbet

This is a lighter alternative to peach ice cream. Very refreshing on a hot summer day.

3 cups water
1 cup sugar
2 cups peaches, peeled and sliced (1 pound)
1/3 cup lemon juice
3/4 cup fresh orange juice

Combine the water and sugar in a medium saucepan. Bring to a boil, and boil for 3 minutes, stirring until the sugar dissolves. Let cool completely.

In the bowl of a food processor, add the peaches, lemon juice, and orange juice. Process until smooth. Combine the peach puree and the chilled sugar syrup, stirring until combined. Pour into a 2-quart ice cream freezer, and follow the manufacturer's directions.

Makes 4 to 6 servings

Note: This recipe could easily be doubled.

strawberry-grapefruit cooler

You can use sugar substitute in this drink.

1 cup whole strawberries, fresh or frozen
1 large grapefruit, peeled and sectioned, retaining any juice
1/4 cup sugar
2 tablespoons honey
1 cup ice cubes

Combine the strawberries, grapefruit and juice, sugar, and honey in a blender. Cover and process until smooth. While the blender is running, add the ice cubes 1 at a time, processing until smooth. Pour into glasses and serve immediately.

Makes 2 servings

FALL HARVEST APPLE CAKE WITH CARAMEL GLAZE

In addition to being delicious, this sure does make your kitchen smell good.

Cake

3 large eggs
1 1/4 cups vegetable oil
2 cups sugar
2 cups all-purpose flour
1 teaspoon baking soda
1 teaspoon salt
1 teaspoon cinnamon
1/2 teaspoon cloves
3 cups apples, peeled and finely chopped
1 1/2 cups pecans or walnuts, chopped
1 1/2 teaspoons vanilla extract

Glaze

1/4 cup butter
1/4 cup heavy whipping cream
1/4 cup sugar
1/4 cup brown sugar
2/3 cup powdered sugar
1/2 teaspoon vanilla extract

To make the cake: Preheat the oven to 350 degrees. Grease and flour a 10-inch tube or Bundt pan.

In the large bowl of an electric mixer, beat the eggs. Add the oil and beat until thick and lemony colored. Beat in the sugar. In a small bowl, mix together the flour, baking soda, and salt. Add to the egg mixture, and mix well. Stir in the cinnamon, cloves, apples, nuts, and vanilla until just combined. Spoon the batter into the prepared pan. Bake 1 hour, or until a toothpick inserted in the center comes out clean. This cake will be very moist. Cool in the pan for 15 minutes before removing to a serving plate.

To make the glaze: Combine the butter, cream, sugar, and brown sugar in an 8-inch iron skillet. Bring to a boil, and boil for 1 minute. Cool to room temperature. Add the powdered sugar and vanilla, and beat until smooth. Drizzle the glaze over the top and sides of the cake.

Makes 16 servings

PiNeapple Applesauce sugar-Free cake

If you need to watch your sugar but still have a sweet tooth, this cake should do the trick for you.

1 (20-ounce) can crushed pineapple, unsweetened
2 cups golden raisins
8 (0.325-ounce) packages artificial sweetener
3/4 cup butter
1 cup unsweetened applesauce
2 large eggs
2 teaspoons vanilla extract
1 1/2 teaspoons cinnamon
1/2 teaspoon cloves
2 cups self-rising flour
1 cup chopped pecans

Preheat the oven to 375 degrees. Grease and flour a 10-inch tube cake pan.

   Drain the pineapple, reserving the liquid. Add enough water to the pineapple juice to equal 2 cups. Combine the juice mixture and the raisins in a medium saucepan. Place over medium heat. Cook until the liquid evaporates, stirring frequently. Add the sweetener, butter, and applesauce. Pour into a large bowl and let cool to lukewarm. Add the eggs and vanilla. Stir to mix well. Add the cinnamon, cloves, and flour. Stir in the pineapple, raisins, and pecans. Pour into the prepared pan.

   Bake 1 hour or until a cake tester inserted in the center comes out clean. Let cool for 10 minutes. Turn out onto a cake plate. Let set at room temperature for 4 hours before serving.

Makes 16 servings

MiNTeD PiNeaPPLe FReeZe

My neighbor Jean Smith keeps this made in the summer and brings it to her neighbors when they are outside doing yard work. I wish everyone were lucky enough to have a neighbor like her.

$1/2$ cup sugar
$1/2$ cup water
$1/4$ teaspoon spearmint extract
3 drops green food coloring
$1/3$ cup lemon juice
$1/2$ cup crushed pineapple
1 cup ginger ale

Mix the sugar, water, mint, and food coloring in a medium saucepan. Place over medium heat and simmer for 10 minutes. Add the lemon juice, pineapple, and ginger ale. Pour into a 9 x 5-inch loaf pan. Place in the freezer.

Freeze until slushy, about 2 hours, and stir with a fork. Keep in the freezer until serving time. Serve in a glass with a spoon.

Makes 4 servings

FLOURLESS PEANUT BUTTER COOKIES WITH PEANUT BUTTER CHIPS

Double the peanut butter flavor.

1 cup brown sugar or brown sugar substitute
1 cup crunchy peanut butter
1 large egg
1 teaspoon baking soda
1 teaspoon vanilla extract
1 cup peanut butter chips

Preheat the oven to 350 degrees. Line a 15 x 15-inch baking sheet with parchment paper.

Mix the brown sugar and peanut butter together in a medium bowl. Stir in the egg, baking soda, and vanilla. Stir in the peanut butter chips. Drop by tablespoonfuls onto the parchment paper. Bake 10 minutes or until puffed. Cool the cookies on the baking sheet. Store in a covered container.

Makes 30 cookies

FROZEN HOT CHOCOLATE

This is just so good. You can also make this almost guilt-free by using low-fat milk and sugar substitute. Dress these up by serving them in your best crystal stemware.

1 1/2 cups light whipping cream
2 tablespoons cocoa powder
1/2 cup sugar
1/2 teaspoon vanilla extract
1/8 teaspoon salt
2 cups ice cubes

Blend the cream, cocoa, sugar, vanilla, and salt in a blender until mixed and the sugar is dissolved. Add the ice cubes and blend until slushy—about 30 seconds or until the ice cubes are finely crushed.

Makes 4 servings

Chapter 6

⊱—✦—⊰

LUCKETTVILLE
BANDS TOGETHER

When Alma Patterson heard that those precious young people over at Luckettville High couldn't afford new band uniforms and might be disqualified from the regional marching competition because of it, she knew there was just one thing to do: host a bake sale.

Alma's mother taught her early on that "to those whom much is given, much is expected," and Alma had made it her mission to look out for the less fortunate. Even when her family didn't have a lot, they shared what they could. Anyone who has lived as long as Alma has knows full well that on any given day, she might be the one who needs help. So she wants people to be ready and willing to return the favor when her time comes. Not that she is keeping score, mind you, just being practical. "Do unto others as you would have them do unto you" is more than the Golden Rule to Alma. It is a way of life.

Although her children have long since graduated from the school (did she mention that her youngest had been head of the drill team?), Alma is still very much community minded, and she cares about decorum.

Alma realized she couldn't do anything about the garish school colors—however much that pained her—but she could at least make sure the uniforms weren't missing tassels or sporting split seams. Last fall when she had gone to watch her grandson play quarterback, she'd liked to have cried when she'd noticed that Myra Robinson's nephew had wrapped a piece of duct tape around the waistband of his pants. It was bad enough that the kid couldn't play the clarinet with any proficiency worth noting, but the ill-fitting uniform added insult to injury. She knew Myra must have been mortified, but Alma didn't mention it because that's the kind of woman she is.

So Alma set out to put on the best bake sale Luckettville had ever seen. Alma trusted that she was just the one to handle such a project, seeing as how she was regarded throughout Clarke County for her organizational and managerial skills. After contacting the school principal—Jack Reynolds knew better than to say no to Alma—and agreeing on a date, Alma got busy drafting a list of the best bakers in town.

It was going to be tricky, though, because some folks fancied themselves to be better cooks than they were in actuality. Please don't get Alma started on the time Edna Fentress promised the library outreach committee she could handle making blueberry crumble for seventy-five when it was time for the annual volunteer appreciation dinner. Alma knew in her gut that those blueberries were from a can even though the stalls down at the farmer's market had been full of fresh, plump jewels at the time.

But Alma didn't want to hurt anyone's feelings—a middle child, she is nothing if not a peacemaker—so she'd decided she'd let anyone who wanted to participate in the bake sale do so. If one of the questionable cooks called her, she just assigned her something simple, like sugar cookies or cornbread sticks. The point of this bake sale was to help the high-school students, not garner culinary acclaim. If Alma could manage to do both, though, where was the harm? She'd called the radio station and asked for a slot on the "Good Neighbor Hour" because Alma appreciates the importance of good publicity. Taking a key lime-lemon cake over to the station just sweetened the deal.

Alma's next call was to Sunny Simpson, a young newcomer to Luckettville who in just a few months had made a name for herself with candy bar cookie pops. The first time Alma had a bite, at the Luckettville Learned Ladies Society's spring fling, she'd almost cried out in ecstasy. Perfection. Sunny's aunt was a highly valued member of the Society, and she had invited Sunny so her twenty-something niece could meet some of Luckettville's upper crust.

"I'd be delighted to help," said Sunny.

That was just the sort of response Alma expected from the fine people of Luckettville. Alma knew Sunny's pops would go fast, and she felt sure she could charge a premium for them. Worth every penny. Around here, what matters is community. If somebody needs help, you offer it, without regard for recognition or reimbursement. Maybe the bake sale would even earn enough to get the cheerleaders some new pom-poms. If memory served, they were looking a little spindly.

Alma was on such a high from her talk with Sunny that she felt brave enough to call Lucinda Evans. Lucinda could be a tough sell, even when the cause was a charitable one. She'd had a hard life, and sometimes Lucinda let her years of disappointment overwhelm her. She could hold on to a grudge longer than anyone Alma had ever known, including her mother-in-law, which is saying something.

Thankfully, Alma caught Lucinda on a good day, a day full of promise instead of regret. So she agreed straightaway to make her German chocolate fried pies. Alma had tasted one of these only once, several years back, and she'd been dreaming of a second chance ever since. Because you never could predict when Lucinda's mood would take a turn, Alma hung up as soon as she could, so as not to give Lucinda time to change her mind.

By the time Alma got off the phone with Lucinda, word had begun to spread about the bake sale. People started reaching out to Alma with offers to bring this or that. Alma took all comers, grateful she lived in such a place full of kind hearted people who wanted to make a difference for those in need. Soon she had a line-up that included pistachio white-chocolate chip cookies, banana butterscotch bread, and peach upside-down cake.

Now that it's all over, even Alma has to admit she was surprised at the success of the bake sale. Not only did they raise enough for new band uniforms, but there was also enough left over to refurbish the cheerleaders' pom-poms and to order a new uniform for the mascot.

Alma just hopes this experience serves as an example to others about what one person can do if she puts her mind to it. She doesn't have time to gloat, though, as she's expected over at the animal shelter. Seems they need to raise money for a new computer, and they've decided Alma is just the gal to help them make it happen.

FRieD BLACKbeRRY Pies

2 cups fresh blackberries
$1/2$ cup sugar
2 tablespoons all-purpose flour
$1/2$ teaspoon cinnamon
Pie crust (see recipe on page 86 for Cherry-Apple Fried Pies)
Oil for frying

In a medium bowl, mix together the blackberries, sugar, flour, and cinnamon. Lightly flour a board, and roll the dough out to $1/4$-inch thick. Cut into 5-inch circles. Place 2 to 3 tablespoons of blackberry filling in the center of each crust round. Brush the top half of the crust with water, and fold over the filling to form a half moon shape. Dip the tines of a fork in flour, and press the edges of the crust together. Prick the top of each pie once to allow steam to escape while cooking.

Fry 2 at a time in a small skillet over medium heat until golden brown, turning once. Drain on a paper towel. Serve warm.

Makes 12 servings

Note: To test if the oil is hot enough, place a small piece of pie crust in the oil. When it begins to fry, remove it and begin frying the pies.

PiNeappLe-Banana Cake

Your guests will love this moist cake.

Cake

3 cups all-purpose flour

1 teaspoon baking soda

1 teaspoon salt

1 teaspoon cinnamon

2 cups sugar

1 1/2 cups vegetable oil

1 teaspoon butter flavoring

3 large eggs, lightly beaten

1 (8-ounce) can crushed pineapple, undrained

2 medium bananas, chopped

2 cups pecans, chopped

Cream Cheese Icing

1/2 cup butter, softened

1 (8-ounce) package cream cheese, softened

1 pound powdered sugar

1 teaspoon vanilla extract

1/2 cup pecans

To make the cake: Preheat the oven to 350 degrees. Grease and flour a 10-inch Bundt pan.

In a large bowl, mix together the flour, baking soda, salt, cinnamon, and sugar. Add the oil, butter flavoring, and eggs, stirring only until moistened. Stir in the pineapple, bananas, and pecans. Spoon the batter into the prepared pan.

Bake 1 hour, or until a cake tester inserted in the center comes out clean. Cool 1 hour before removing from the pan. Ice with the cream cheese icing. Refrigerate leftovers.

To make the icing: Beat the butter and cream cheese in a mixing bowl until light. Add the powdered sugar gradually and beat until fluffy. Stir in the vanilla and pecans.

Makes 14 to 16 servings

FRIED PECAN PIES WITH WHITE CHOCOLATE CHIPS

$1/2$ cup brown sugar
1 tablespoon all-purpose flour
1 large egg, beaten
$1/2$ cup light corn syrup
2 tablespoons butter
$1/2$ cup pecans, toasted and chopped
$1/8$ teaspoon salt
$1/2$ cup white chocolate chips
Pie crust (see recipe on page 86 for Cherry-Apple Fried Pies)
Oil for frying

Combine the brown sugar, flour, and egg in a medium saucepan. Stir to mix well. Add the corn syrup, butter, pecans, and salt. Place over medium-low heat. Bring to a boil, stirring constantly. Boil 2 minutes.

Let mixture get cold. Stir in the white chocolate chips. Lightly flour a board, and roll the dough out to $1/4$ -inch thick. Cut into 5-inch circles. Place a tablespoon of filling onto each circle of dough. Brush the top half of the round with water, and fold over the filling to form a half-moon shape. Dip the tines of a fork in flour, and press the edges of the crust together. Prick the top of each pie once to allow the steam to escape during cooking.

Fry 2 at a time in a small skillet over medium heat until golden brown, turning once. Drain on a paper towel. Serve warm.

Makes 12 pies

Note: To test if the oil is hot enough, place a small piece of pie crust in the oil. When it begins to fry, remove it and begin frying the pies.

Best-Thing-You-Ever-Put-In-Your-Mouth Yellow Cake with Chocolate Cream Cheese Icing

This is the most moist cake I have ever made. It is my go-to cake because it's so easy to make and tastes so good.

Cake

2 1/4 cups all-purpose flour

2 1/2 teaspoons baking powder

1 teaspoon salt

1 1/2 cups sugar

3/4 cup shortening

3/4 cup milk

3 large eggs

1 teaspoon vanilla extract

Chocolate Cream Cheese Icing

2 (8-ounce) packages cream cheese, softened

2 (1 pound) packages powdered sugar

1/4 cup cocoa

1 teaspoon vanilla extract

To make the cake: Preheat the oven to 350 degrees. Grease and flour two 9-inch cake pans.

In a large mixing bowl, combine the flour, baking powder, salt, sugar, shortening, milk, eggs, and vanilla. Cream together with an electric mixer at low speed until blended. Beat at medium speed for 5 minutes until fluffy. Divide between the greased and floured pans.

Bake 20 to 25 minutes until golden brown, or until a cake tester inserted in the center comes out clean. Cool for 10 minutes. Remove from the pans and cool completely before icing.

To make the icing: In a large mixing bowl, beat the cream cheese with an electric mixer until fluffy. Gradually add the powdered sugar and cocoa, beating until blended. Stir in the vanilla.

Spread the icing between the layers and on the top and sides of the cooled cake. Keep refrigerated.

Makes 16 servings

GRAHAM CRACKER CAKE WITH PINEAPPLE LEMON FILLING, AND CREAM CHEESE FROSTING

I carried this to church supper awhile back and there wasn't a crumb left over.

Cake

1 cup butter, softened

1 1/2 cups sugar

5 large eggs

3/4 cup milk

1 (13.5-ounce) box graham cracker crumbs

2 teaspoons vanilla extract

1/4 teaspoon salt

2 teaspoons baking powder

1 cup pecans, chopped

1 cup flaked coconut

Filling

1 cup sugar

3 tablespoons all-purpose flour

1 (20-ounce) can crushed pineapple, partially drained

1/3 cup lemon juice

1/4 cup butter, melted

Frosting

1/2 cup butter, softened

1 (8-ounce) package cream cheese, softened

1 pound powdered sugar

2 teaspoons vanilla extract

1/8 teaspoon salt

1/2 cup pecans, chopped

To make the cake: Preheat the oven to 325 degrees. Grease and line four 8-inch round cake pans with wax paper.

In the bowl of an electric mixer, cream the butter and sugar together. Add the eggs one at a time, beating well after each addition. Add the milk, graham cracker crumbs, vanilla, salt, and baking powder. Mix well. Stir in the pecans and coconut. Divide among the prepared pans.

Bake 30 to 35 minutes or until a cake tester inserted in the center comes out clean. Cool completely before filling and frosting.

To make the filling: Combine the sugar, flour, and pineapple in a medium saucepan. Place over medium heat, adding the lemon juice and butter, stirring to combine. Bring to a boil, stirring constantly. Boil 3 minutes. Let cool completely before adding to cake layers.

To make the frosting: In a medium bowl, cream the butter and cream cheese together. Add the powdered sugar, vanilla, and salt. Mix well. Stir in the chopped pecans.

To assemble: Place one cake on a cake plate, spread with the pineapple filling. Stack the second cake on top of the first and add another layer of filling. Repeat with the third cake. Place the fourth cake on top. Frost the top and sides of the cakes with the cream cheese frosting. Let set for 2 hours at room temperature prior to slicing. Refrigerate leftovers.

Makes 16 servings

Banana Butterscotch Bread

Everybody has a banana bread recipe they love. The butterscotch surprise kicks this up a notch and has made it a recipe that many of my friends have requested over the years.

1 $3/4$ cups all-purpose flour
2 teaspoons baking powder
$1/2$ teaspoon baking soda
$1/2$ teaspoon salt
1 teaspoon cinnamon
1 cup mashed ripe bananas (2 medium)
$3/4$ cup sugar
2 large eggs
$1/4$ cup butter, melted
$1/4$ cup milk
1 cup butterscotch morsels
1 cup pecans, chopped and divided

Preheat the oven to 350 degrees. Grease a 9 x 5 x 3-inch loaf pan and line the bottom with greased waxed paper.

Combine the flour, baking powder, baking soda, salt, and cinnamon in a large mixing bowl and set aside. In a small bowl, mix the bananas, sugar, eggs, and butter. Alternately add the banana mixture and the milk to the flour mixture, beating with an electric mixer. Stir in the butterscotch morsels and $2/3$ cup of the pecans. Spoon the batter into the prepared pan. Sprinkle with the remaining $1/3$ cup of pecans.

Bake 45 to 50 minutes or until a cake tester inserted in the center comes out clean. Cool for 20 minutes before removing from pan.

Makes 12 to14 servings

Key Lime-Lemon Cake

What I like best about this cake is the combination of the key lime and lemon.

Cake
1 (18-ounce) package lemon cake mix
1 (3-ounce) package lemon instant pudding mix
4 large eggs
1 cup vegetable oil
3/4 cup water
1/4 cup key lime juice

Key Lime Glaze
2 cups powdered sugar
1/3 cup key lime juice
2 tablespoons water
3 tablespoons butter, softened
Sliced limes and strawberries for garnish

To make the cake: Preheat the oven to 350 degrees. Grease and flour a 10-inch Bundt pan.

In a large bowl, combine the cake mix, pudding mix, eggs, oil, water, and lime juice. Beat at medium speed for 2 minutes with an electric mixer. Spoon the batter into the prepared pan. Bake 55 minutes to 1 hour, or until a cake tester inserted in the center comes out clean. Cool in the pan for 20 minutes. Remove to a cake plate before glazing.

To make the glaze: Combine the powdered sugar, lime juice, water, and butter in a medium mixing bowl and beat until smooth. Drizzle over the warm cake. Garnish with limes and strawberries.

Makes 16 servings

JUANITA'S DEVIL'S FOOD CAKE WITH CHOCOLATE ICING

This recipe came from my late sister, Juanita. The name is a little ironic because her husband was a preacher.

Cake
1/2 cup butter, softened
1 1/3 cups sugar
2 large eggs
3 tablespoons cocoa powder
2 tablespoons water
2 cups all-purpose flour
3/4 teaspoon salt
1 teaspoon baking soda

1 cup buttermilk
1 teaspoon vanilla extract

Chocolate Icing
2 cups sugar
3 tablespoons cocoa powder
1/2 cup milk
1/2 cup butter, softened

To make the cake: Preheat the oven to 350 degrees. Butter and flour two 8-inch cake pans.

Place the butter in the bowl of an electric mixer. Add the sugar, mixing well on medium speed. Add the eggs. In a small bowl, mix the cocoa and water to make a paste. Add the paste to the butter mixture. In a small bowl, mix the flour and salt together. In another small bowl, combine the baking soda and buttermilk. Alternately add the flour mixture and the buttermilk mixture to the cake batter, beginning and ending with the flour. Mix in the vanilla. Divide between the two pie pans.

Bake 20 to 25 minutes or until a cake tester inserted in the center comes out clean. Cool in the pans for 5 minutes. Remove from the pans and cool completely before icing.

To make the icing: Mix the sugar and cocoa together in a medium saucepan. Stir in the milk until the sugar and cocoa are dissolved. Add the butter. Place over medium heat and bring to a rolling boil, stirring constantly. Boil 1 minute. Remove from the heat and let cool for 3 to 5 minutes. Beat with a mixer or spoon until the icing begins to thicken.

To assemble: Place 1 cake on the serving plate, and put a small amount of icing in the middle of the cake. Place the second cake on top, and ice the top and sides. This icing will harden quickly.

Makes 12 to 16 servings

CANDY BAR COOKIE POPS

Your kids and grandkids will love these. Mine do.

1/2 cup sugar
1/2 cup brown sugar, firmly packed
1/2 cup butter, softened
1/2 cup peanut butter
1 teaspoon vanilla extract
1 large egg
1 1/2 cups all-purpose flour
1/2 teaspoon baking soda
1/2 teaspoon baking powder
1/4 teaspoon salt
16 wooden popsicle sticks
16 fun-size Snickers

Preheat the oven to 375 degrees. In a large bowl, combine the sugar, brown sugar, butter, peanut butter, vanilla, and egg. Cream well on low speed with an electric mixer. Add the flour, baking soda, baking powder, and salt, continuing to mix until the dry ingredients are fully incorporated. Insert a wooden stick into each candy bar. Using your hands, form 1/4 cup of the cookie dough around the candy bar, completely covering it so that the surface is smooth.

On a large ungreased cookie sheet, place the pops 6 inches apart, allowing room for the sticks and for each cookie to spread. Each cookie will be 4 inches round after baking. Bake 14 minutes or until golden brown. Cool completely. At this time you may wrap each cookie in plastic wrap and tie with a ribbon. That is, if they last that long.

Makes 16 pops

Peach-Coconut Upside-Down Cake

This is quite similar to a pineapple upside-down cake, but I honestly think this one is better. It is one of my new favorite dishes.

1/2 cup butter
1 cup brown sugar
1 1/2 tablespoons light corn syrup
1 1/2 cups flaked coconut
1 (16-ounce) can peach slices, drained
1 1/2 cups all-purpose flour
1 cup sugar
1/3 teaspoon salt
2 teaspoons baking powder
6 tablespoons shortening
2 large eggs
3/4 cup milk
3/4 teaspoon vanilla extract

Preheat the oven to 375 degrees. Melt the butter in a 10-inch iron skillet. Stir in the brown sugar, corn syrup, and coconut. Spread to evenly cover the bottom of the skillet. Arrange the peach slices, cut side up, over the mixture.

In a mixing bowl, sift together the flour, sugar, salt, and baking powder. Add the shortening, eggs, milk, and vanilla. Mix on medium speed for 2 minutes. Spread the batter over the peach-coconut mixture.

Bake 30 to 35 minutes or until a wooden toothpick inserted in the middle of the cake comes out clean. Cool for 2 minutes. Turn onto a large serving plate. Store, covered, at room temperature.

Makes 10 servings

GERMAN CHOCOLATE FRIED PIES

1/4 cup sugar
1 1/2 tablespoons cornstarch
3/4 cup milk
2 ounces German chocolate bar
1 large egg yolk, beaten
1 tablespoon butter
1/2 cup coconut
1/2 cup pecans, chopped
1 teaspoon vanilla extract
Pie crust (see recipe on page 86 for Cherry-Apple Fried Pies)
Oil for frying

Mix the sugar, cornstarch, and milk together in a small saucepan. Add the chocolate bar and beaten egg yolk. Cook over medium heat, stirring constantly, until the mixture comes to a boil and thickens. Remove from the heat, and add the butter, coconut, pecans, and vanilla, stirring to mix well. Cover with plastic wrap and cool completely before using.

Roll the dough to 3/4-inch thickness. Cut into 5-inch rounds. Place 1 1/2 tablespoons of filling in the center. Brush the edges with water and press together. Prick the top of each pie with a fork. Fry the pies in 1/2 inch of oil for 2 to 3 minutes per side.

Makes 12 servings

Note: To test if the oil is hot enough, place a small piece of pie crust in the oil. When it begins to fry, remove it and begin frying the pies.

GERMAN CHOCOLATE CAKE ROLL

If I had to name my favorite cake, it would have to be German chocolate. This is a fun variation on the traditional classic.

Filling

1 (14-ounce) can sweetened condensed milk

2 large egg yolks

2/3 cup flaked coconut

3/4 cup chopped pecans

1/4 cup butter, melted

1 teaspoon vanilla extract

Cake

3 large eggs

1 cup sugar

1 teaspoon vanilla extract

2/3 cup all-purpose flour

1/4 cup cocoa powder

1/8 teaspoon salt

1/3 cup water

Powdered sugar for dusting

Glaze

1/3 cup semi-sweet chocolate chips

3 tablespoons butter

1/2 teaspoon vanilla extract

To make the filling: Line a 15 x 10 x 1-inch jelly roll pan with parchment paper. Spray or grease the paper.

In a medium bowl, combine the condensed milk, egg yolks, coconut, pecans, butter, and vanilla, mixing well. Spread evenly onto the prepared baking pan.

To make the cake: Preheat the oven to 350 degrees. In a large bowl, beat the eggs at high speed with an electric mixer until fluffy. Gradually beat in the sugar, continuing to beat for 2 minutes. Add the vanilla, flour, cocoa, salt, and water, and continue to beat for 1 minute. Pour evenly over the coconut-milk mixture.

Bake 25 minutes or until the cake springs back when lightly touched. Sprinkle generously with powdered sugar, and immediately turn onto a tea towel. Peel off the parchment paper. While still warm, beginning at the narrow end, roll up the cake, jelly-roll fashion. Place on a serving plate seam side down to cool.

To make the glaze: In a small saucepan over low heat, melt the semi-sweet chocolate chips with the butter. Stir until smooth. Remove from the heat and stir in the vanilla. Drizzle over the cake. Sprinkle with additional powdered sugar, if desired.

Makes 10 servings

WHITE CHOCOLATE CHIP AND PISTACHIO OATMEAL COOKIES

Pistachios are one of my favorite nuts to cook with. They really add a lot to these cookies.

1 cup butter, softened
1/4 cup shortening
1 cup brown sugar, firmly packed
1/2 cup sugar
2 large eggs
2 teaspoons vanilla extract
2 cups all-purpose flour
1/2 cup whole wheat flour
1 teaspoon baking soda
1 teaspoon baking powder
1/8 teaspoon salt
1/2 cup oats
1 (11-ounce) package white chocolate chips
2 cups roasted pistachios, coarsely chopped

Preheat the oven to 350 degrees. In a large bowl, cream the butter, shortening, brown sugar, and sugar with an electric mixer until creamy. Add the eggs and vanilla. In a medium bowl, mix together the flour, whole wheat flour, baking soda, baking powder, salt, and oats. Gradually add the dry mixture to the batter. When fully incorporated, stir in the chocolate chips and pistachios. Chill for 45 minutes prior to baking.

Drop by tablespoonfuls 2 inches apart on a large ungreased cookie sheet. Bake 8 minutes. Let cool 2 minutes before removing to a wire rack to cool completely.

Makes 48 to 60 cookies

WHITE CHOCOLATE COCONUT CAKE WITH COCONUT FILLING, AND BOILED ICING,

This cake always brings a lot of money when I donate it to a bake sale or charity auction.

Cake
3/4 cup white chocolate chips
1/2 cup water
1 cup butter, softened
2 cups sugar, divided
4 large eggs, separated
1 teaspoon vanilla extract
2 1/2 cups cake flour, sifted
1 1/2 teaspoons baking powder
1/2 teaspoon salt
1 cup buttermilk
1 cup chopped pecans
1 cup flaked coconut

Coconut Filling
1 1/4 cups sugar
2 cups water
2 1/2 cups sweetened flaked coconut

Boiled Frosting
1/2 cup water
3 cups sugar
1/4 cup light corn syrup
4 large egg whites
1/2 teaspoon cream of tartar
1 teaspoon almond extract
1 teaspoon vanilla extract
1/2 cup powdered sugar

To make the cake: Preheat the oven to 350 degrees. Grease and flour three 9-inch cake pans.

Melt the white chocolate chips with water in the top of a double boiler over low heat. Stir to melt. Set aside to cool. Cream the butter with 1 1/2 cups sugar in the bowl of an electric mixer until fluffy. Add the egg yolks one at a time, continuing to beat well. Add the vanilla and the melted and cooled chocolate mixture. In a medium bowl, sift the flour, baking powder, and salt together. Add the flour alternately with the buttermilk to the chocolate mixture. Fold in the chopped pecans and coconut with a rubber spatula. Beat the egg whites until soft peaks form, and gradually fold in the remaining 1/2 cup sugar. Fold the egg whites into the cake batter. Divide among the three cake pans. Bake 25 to 30 minutes or until a cake tester inserted in the center comes out clean. Let the cakes cool.

To make the filling: Mix the sugar and water together in a large saucepan. Bring to a boil over medium heat for 1 minute. Add the coconut and bring to a boil again, this time for 3 minutes. Spoon the filling over the cooled cake layers and stack.

To make the frosting: In a large saucepan, stir together the water, sugar, and syrup until the sugar is dissolved. Place over medium-high heat. Bring to a boil, and continue to cook until the mixture reaches 238 degrees on a candy thermometer, stirring occasionally. Beat the egg whites and cream of tartar in the bowl of an electric mixer until stiff. Slowly pour the cooked syrup over the egg whites, continuing to beat until smooth. Add the almond extract, vanilla, and powdered sugar, beating until all is dissolved. Spread over the top and sides of the cake. Let set 2 hours before serving.

Makes 16 servings

MiLKY WaY PeCaN PollND CaKe

This recipe had to have been created by the angels for people with a sweet tooth.

12 1/2 ounces Milky Way candy bars
1 cup butter, divided
1 1/2 cups sugar
4 large eggs
2 1/2 cups all-purpose flour
1/2 teaspoon baking soda
1/4 teaspoon salt
1 1/4 cups buttermilk
1 teaspoon vanilla extract
2 cups chopped pecans

Preheat the oven to 350 degrees. Grease and flour a 10-inch Bundt pan.

Combine the candy bars with 1/2 cup butter in a saucepan and melt over low heat, stirring occasionally. While the candy is melting, cream 1/2 cup butter and sugar in the bowl of an electric mixer until light. Add the eggs one at a time, beating well after each addition. In a small bowl, mix the flour, baking soda, and salt. Add the dry ingredients alternately with the buttermilk. Mix until smooth. Add the melted candy mixture, and continue mixing. Stir in the vanilla and pecans. Pour the batter into the prepared pan.

Bake 1 hour, or until a cake tester inserted in the center comes out clean. Let cool in the pan for 20 minutes. Remove from the pan and allow to cool completely. Cover and store at room temperature.

Makes 16 to 20 servings

Note: It doesn't really matter what size candy bar you use as long as the end weight is 12 1/2 ounces.

Chapter 7

❧—❧

HONEY'S SWEET TOOTH

Not long after Honey Holcomb became famous around Luckettville for her spectacular petit fours, she dreamed of opening her own bakery. She'd been reading in *Southern Living* about shops that specialized in cupcakes opening up around the South, and she thought, *If they can do it, so can I.* But Honey didn't like to be pigeonholed, so she wasn't going to stop there. Her bakery would also offer cakes, pies, muffins, scones, and something called whoopie pies too.

Although Honey did not really consider herself the kind of woman who cared about material things, she calculated that by charging three to four dollars a cupcake, there was money to be made. Once Honey put her mind to something, you were better off just to hide and watch. Goodness knows, with her youngest child in desperate need of braces and the oldest threatening to apply to a private college out of state, she and her better half, Dale, could use all the extra cash they could find. But her main motivation was personal fulfillment. Honey had vowed long ago not to be one of those people who had regrets on her deathbed. Honey Holcomb was going out on top.

As happens with some of the best things in life, Honey had come to professional baking quite by accident. Her original motivation had been simply to prove to her sister that she could do it, and then the thing had just mushroomed. After Honey made petit fours for her niece's engagement party, almost overnight she became known for her perfectly shaped squares of flour and sugar. Some, like Dale, might even say she was sought after. When she was featured on the local access channel for a documentary on the lost art of icing, she started getting requests to make more and more petit fours for all kinds of parties around town. Honey hadn't been in demand like this since the fourth grade, when her father got a promotion and bought an aboveground pool for the backyard. Honey was secretly hoping her newfound popularity would last longer than her grade-school reign.

Last month, when the junior college called and asked her to make five hundred petit fours for the graduation reception, iced with the school's colors of blue and green, Honey knew she had hit on something big. She'd had to use ovens all over the neighborhood to pull that one off, but she had done it. When the college president singled her out for her efforts, Honey had to admit she felt special.

True, she is a Leo, and she appreciates being noticed on occasion. But it isn't essential to her, not really, not like it is with Debbie Driscoll, who continued to wear short, form-fitting dresses long after it was seemly to do so. Sometimes there were even sequins involved. Bless her heart. Honey feels sorry for her, really, because Debbie seems so desperate. Word around town is that Debbie has practically thrown herself at the new preacher over at All Souls Chapel even though she is twenty years his senior if she is a day.

Since Annabelle's Bakery shut down after Annabelle went to California to live with her daughter; Honey thinks she can snatch up the space on the Square without any trouble. Everyone thought Annabelle would be back after her hip healed, but Honey has it on good authority that Annabelle's daughter has decided her mother is staying put. Apparently Happy Trails Retirement Village isn't good enough for the likes of Annabelle's momma. (Did Honey say that out loud?)

So the bakery space will be coming up for rent any day now. Honey knows it will be hers, just as sure as she knows her eyes are green and her hips are wide. She isn't being presumptuous, or cocky, just confident. Honey has been determined all her life—you have to be when your sister is described as "the pretty one" and you're labeled "good personality"—and she isn't about to hold back now. She can practically taste the sweetness of success already.

Sure enough, she is soon ordering the sign for Honey's Sweet Tooth and mailing invitations for the grand opening. She plans to offer free samples and reduced prices during her first week. Dale warns her not to give too much away, but Honey knows her generosity will pay off.

She starts making samples of everything from strawberry shortcake cupcakes to fig muffins, surprise coconut pie to apple dumplings with cheddar cheese pastry. She has them all taste tested because she fears Dale

won't tell her the truth. Sometimes he lets his love for Honey get in the way of honesty, like the time he told her that floral skirt was flattering when in fact it made her look like her Aunt Tilda's tea cozy.

"You always look beautiful to me," he said when she called him on it, after her sister made her promise never to leave the house in that outfit again.

So only after ten people Honey can't claim as kin sign off on the desserts does she consider them good enough to sell at Honey's Sweet Tooth.

And sell they do. Before she knows it, Honey has to hire more assistants and extend her hours on Friday and Saturday. Who knows? Maybe one day her little shop will grow to be a franchise, with bakeries all across the state. Honey has long suspected that all those *A*s she earned in home economics would come in handy, despite what her sister had said at the time—that being skilled with a spatula was nothing to be proud of.

Honey would like to go on and on, but she's got a big order to prepare. After being spurned by Reverend Boydston, Debbie Driscoll managed to snag a widower out at the Happy Trails Retirement Village. Honey's in charge of the reception, and she has to get started on the cake. Debbie wants basket weave.

"Hope springs eternal," Debbie had said when she called to tell Honey the good news.

Indeed it does, thinks Honey, as she slips an apron around her neck, then ties it at her waist. Indeed it does.

STRAWBERRY SHORTCAKE CUPCAKES

1/2 cup butter, softened
1/2 cup sugar
2 large eggs
1 cup self-rising flour
1/2 teaspoon baking powder
1/2 teaspoon vanilla extract
3 tablespoons strawberry preserves
1 cup frozen whipped topping, thawed
12 large strawberries, sliced
Powdered sugar for dusting

Preheat the oven to 350 degrees. Line a 12-cup cupcake pan with paper liners.

Cream the butter and sugar together until fluffy, using an electric mixer. Beat in the eggs one at a time. In a small bowl, combine the flour and baking powder. Fold the flour mixture into the egg mixture. Stir in the vanilla. Fill each lined cup 2/3 full. Bake 15 to 18 minutes or until golden brown. Cool completely.

To decorate, carefully slice away 1/2 inch of the top of each cupcake. Reserve. Spread each cupcake with 2 teaspoons of preserves and a dollop of whipped topping. Garnish with a strawberry slice. Replace the top of each cupcake. Sprinkle with powdered sugar.

Makes 12 servings

FRESH FROZEN RASPBERRY YOGURT

A perfect summer day treat.

1 1/2 pounds fresh red raspberries
1 1/2 cups sugar substitute
1/4 cup lemon juice
1 cup low-fat milk
3 cups plain low-fat yogurt

Place the raspberries, sugar substitute, and lemon juice in a food processor. Blend on high speed until smooth. Strain through a mesh sieve, if you desire. Pour the raspberry mixture in a large mixing bowl. Stir in the milk and yogurt. Place in an ice cream freezer, and freeze according to the manufacturer's directions.

Makes 6 servings

APPLE AND CRANBERRY MUFFINS WITH WALNUTS

The year-round availability of dried cranberries means these delicious muffins are something you can enjoy anytime the mood hits.

3 $1/2$ cups all-purpose flour

3 cups peeled and finely chopped apples

2 cups sugar

1 teaspoon salt

1 teaspoon baking soda

$3/4$ cup dried cranberries

1 $1/2$ teaspoons cinnamon

1 $1/2$ cups vegetable oil

2 large eggs, slightly beaten

1 cup chopped walnuts

1 $1/2$ teaspoons vanilla extract

Preheat the oven to 350 degrees. Lightly grease or line with paper two 12-cup muffin tins.

In a large bowl, combine the flour, apples, sugar, salt, baking soda, cranberries, and cinnamon. Stir in the oil, eggs, walnuts, and vanilla. The batter will be stiff. Fill each muffin tin $2/3$ full. Bake 20 to 25 minutes, or until a toothpick inserted in the center of each muffin comes out clean.

Makes 24 servings

Randy's Favorite Banana Split Pie

I was sure blessed with a good son-in-law. He is wonderful to my daughter and my grandchildren, and he loves to eat. This is his favorite.

1 (8-ounce) package cream cheese, softened
1 cup powdered sugar
1/3 cup milk
1 (9-inch) chocolate pie crust
2 medium bananas, sliced
1 (8-ounce) can crushed pineapple, drained
1 (8-ounce) carton whipped topping, thawed
1 (6-ounce) bottle maraschino cherries, drained
1/2 cup pecans, finely chopped

In a medium bowl, mix together the cream cheese, powdered sugar, and milk. Pour the mixture into the chocolate crust. Top with the sliced bananas. Add the crushed pineapple. Spread with the whipped topping. Garnish with maraschino cherries, and sprinkle with pecans. Refrigerate for 4 hours or overnight.

Makes 6 to 8 servings

Lemon-Raspberry Cupcakes with Lemon Icing

These cupcakes look like spring—but you can enjoy them all year long.

Cupcakes
2 cups all-purpose flour
1 cup sugar
1 tablespoon baking powder
$1/2$ teaspoon salt
1 cup light whipping cream
$1/2$ cup vegetable oil
1 teaspoon lemon extract
2 large eggs
1 $1/2$ cups fresh raspberries

Lemon Icing
2 cups powdered sugar
$1/3$ cup butter, softened
2 teaspoons lemon zest
2 tablespoons lemon juice

To make the cupcakes: Preheat the oven to 350 degrees. Line 18 cupcake cups with paper liners.

Mix together the flour, sugar, baking powder, and salt in a large mixing bowl. Set aside. In a small bowl, combine the cream, vegetable oil, lemon extract, and eggs, whisking to blend. Stir the liquid ingredients into the dry mixture, and mix well. Fold in the raspberries. Fill each cup $2/3$ full.

Bake 20 to 25 minutes, or until golden brown and a toothpick inserted in the center of each cupcake comes out clean. Cool completely before icing.

To make the icing: Cream together the powdered sugar, butter, lemon zest, and lemon juice with an electric mixer. Mix until thoroughly blended, about 3 minutes. Spread over the tops of the cooled cupcakes.

Makes 18 cupcakes

PiNK LeMoNaDe CupCakes

Cupcakes

1 cup self-rising flour
$2/3$ cup sugar
4 tablespoons butter, softened
$1/3$ cup frozen pink lemonade concentrate, thawed (reserve some for the frosting)
$1/4$ cup buttermilk
1 large egg
$1/2$ teaspoon vanilla extract
3 drops of red food coloring

Lemonade Butter Frosting

2 cups powdered sugar
5 tablespoons butter, softened
2 tablespoons pink lemonade concentrate (leftover from the cupcake ingredient)
1 tablespoon light whipping cream
2 drops red food coloring

To make the cupcakes: Preheat the oven to 350 degrees. Line 12 muffin tin cups with paper liners. In a small bowl, use an electric mixer to combine the flour, sugar, and butter on low speed until you get a sandy mixture. Add the lemonade, buttermilk, egg, and vanilla, and beat at medium speed until well combined. Add the food coloring, stirring until thoroughly mixed. Scoop the batter into the paper liners ($2/3$ full). Bake 20 to 25 minutes or until the tops spring back when lightly touched. Let cool completely before frosting.

To make the frosting: In a medium mixing bowl, add the sugar, butter, lemonade, and cream. Using an electric mixer, beat until the frosting is fluffy. Add the food coloring, continuing to mix until the color is uniformly pink. Spread on the cooled cupcakes.

Makes 12 servings

Whoopie Pecan Pies

I have taught several of my cooking class students how to make this treat. It is always a big hit and one that they can easily make at home for their own family and friends.

Pies

2 cups all-purpose flour
1/4 cup cocoa powder
1 1/4 teaspoons baking soda
1 teaspoon salt
1 cup buttermilk
1 teaspoon vanilla extract
1/2 cup butter, softened
1 cup brown sugar, firmly packed
1 large egg

Filling

1/2 cup butter, softened
2 cups powdered sugar
1 (7-ounce) jar marshmallow cream
1 teaspoon vanilla extract
1/2 cup pecans, finely chopped

To make the pies: Preheat the oven to 350 degrees. Lightly grease 2 large cookie sheets.

Mix the flour, cocoa, baking soda, and salt in a small bowl and set aside. Mix the buttermilk and vanilla together in a small bowl and set aside. Place the butter and brown sugar in the bowl of an electric mixer, and cream together for 3 minutes. Add the egg and continue to mix. Add the flour mixture and buttermilk mixture alternately, beginning and ending with the dry mix. Mix until smooth. Spoon 2 tablespoons of batter about 2 inches apart onto the greased baking pan. Bake 10 to 12 minutes. Cool completely before filling.

To make the filling: In a large bowl, cream together the butter, sugar, marshmallow cream, vanilla, and pecans with an electric mixer until smooth. When the pies are cool, spread the filling on the flat side of half of the pies. Top with the remaining pies, flat side down.

Makes 12 to 14 servings

Caramel-Dipped Apples with Chocolate and Pecans

These apples are a real treat any time of year, not just Halloween. I slice each apple into eight wedges and serve them that way. If you slice the apples, either serve them immediately or sprinkle with lemon juice to keep them from turning brown.

1 (14-ounce) package caramels
2 tablespoons water
4 medium apples (your favorite)
4 wooden sticks
1 (11-ounce) package semi-sweet chocolate chips, melted
1 (11-ounce) package white chocolate chips, melted
1 cup pecans, finely chopped

Butter a large piece of waxed paper. In the double boiler over medium heat, melt the caramels and water together. Place the wooden stick in the stem end of each apple. Dip in the melted caramel, turning until coated. Place on the buttered wax paper. Let stand until the caramel is firm. Drizzle with the melted dark and white chocolate. Sprinkle with chopped pecans. Refrigerate 2 hours before serving.

Makes 4 servings

Note: You could substitute peanuts for the pecans or use different colored sprinkles or graham cracker crumbs for a little variety.

SCOTT'S CHOCOLATE CHIP CAKE

This is the cake my grandson wants and gets every year on his birthday.

1 (18.25-ounce) box yellow cake mix
1 (3-ounce) box vanilla instant pudding
1/2 cup vegetable oil
1/2 cup water
4 large eggs
1 (8-ounce) carton sour cream
1 cup semi-sweet chocolate chips

Preheat the oven to 350 degrees. Grease and flour a 10-inch Bundt pan.

Mix the cake mix and instant pudding in a large bowl with an electric mixer. Add the oil, water, eggs, and sour cream. Beat at medium speed for 2 minutes. Stop and scrape down the bowl. Mix for 1 more minute. Stir in the chocolate chips. Pour into the Bundt pan.

Bake 35 to 40 minutes, or until a cake tester inserted in the center comes out clean. Let cool 5 minutes in the pan before turning out onto a cake plate.

Makes 16 servings

MISS IRENE'S APPLE DUMPLINGS WITH CHEDDAR CHEESE PASTRY

My mother, Miss Irene, was the queen of apple dumplings. She made them all the time, and I think of her every time I make these.

Dumplings

2 cups all-purpose flour

1 teaspoon salt

1 cup grated cheddar cheese

2/3 cup shortening

6 to 7 tablespoons ice water

2 tablespoons butter

1/2 cup sugar

1 teaspoon cinnamon

6 medium granny smith apples, peeled and cored

Syrup

1 cup sugar

2 cups water

1/2 teaspoon cinnamon

1/4 cup butter, softened

To make the dumplings: Mix the flour, salt, and cheese together in a large mixing bowl. Cut in the shortening with a pastry blender or your fingers until the mixture is blended. Add the water 1 tablespoon at a time, mixing with a fork until the flour is moistened. Gather into a ball. Roll the pastry 1/8-inch thick. Cut into six 6-inch squares. In a small bowl, mix the butter, sugar, and cinnamon to a paste. Divide equally among the 6 apples, spooning into the center of each apple.

Place 1 apple in the center of each square. Moisten the edges with water. Pinch up the edges of the dough around the apples to seal, and then prick with a fork. Set the apples aside while you prepare the syrup.

To make the syrup: Preheat the oven to 450 degrees. Lightly butter a 13 x 9-inch baking pan.

Combine the sugar, water, cinnamon, and butter in a saucepan. Bring to a boil, and cook for 3 minutes, stirring occasionally. Place the dumplings in the baking pan, and pour the syrup over them. Bake 10 minutes. Reduce the heat to 325 degrees, and continue to bake for 45 minutes or until the dumplings are golden brown. Serve warm.

Makes 6 servings

PISTACHIO PUDDING CAKE

This has been a favorite of mine for many years. This green cake is perfect for St. Patrick's Day.

1 (18.25-ounce) box white cake mix
3 large eggs
3/4 cup vegetable oil
1/2 cup pistachios, chopped
2 (3-ounce) packages pistachio instant pudding mix, divided
1 cup lemon-lime soda
1/2 cup flaked coconut
1 teaspoon coconut flavoring
1 (8-ounce) carton frozen whipped topping, thawed

Preheat the oven to 350 degrees. Grease and flour a 13 x 9-inch baking pan.

In a large bowl, combine the cake mix, eggs, oil, pistachios, one package of the pistachio pudding mix, lemon-lime soda, coconut, and coconut flavoring. Mix at medium speed with an electric mixer for 2 minutes. Pour the batter into the prepared pan.

Bake 30 to 35 minutes, or until a cake tester inserted in the center comes out clean. Cool completely.

Mix the thawed topping and 1 package of instant pistachio pudding together. Spread over the cooled cake. Chill until ready to serve.

Makes 16 servings

STRAWBERRY CAKE WITH STRAWBERRY FROSTING

This is my son Bryan's cake of choice on his birthday.

Cake

1 (18.25-ounce) box white cake mix
1 (3-ounce) box strawberry Jell-O
1/2 cup milk
1 cup vegetable oil
4 large eggs
1 cup fresh strawberries, diced
1 cup pecans, chopped

Strawberry Frosting

1/2 cup butter, softened
1 pound powdered sugar
1/2 cup fresh strawberries
1/2 cup pecans, chopped

To make the cake: Preheat the oven to 350 degrees. Grease and flour a 13 x 9-inch baking pan.

Pour the cake mix and Jell-O into a large bowl. Add the milk, oil, and eggs, and beat on medium speed for 3 minutes with an electric mixer. Stir in the strawberries and pecans. Pour the batter into the baking dish.

Bake 35 to 40 minutes, or until a toothpick inserted in the center comes out clean. Let cool and top with frosting.

To make the frosting: In a large bowl, cream the butter with the powdered sugar. Mix in the strawberries and pecans. Spread over the cake. Cover and refrigerate any leftovers.

Makes 12 to 14 servings

Big Easy Blueberry Beignets with White Chocolate Sauce

No matter where you live, these will remind you of New Orleans.

Beignets

3/4 cup water

1 tablespoon sugar plus 1/3 cup sugar, divided

1/2 cup evaporated milk

1 package dry yeast

3 1/2 cups all-purpose flour

1 large egg

2 tablespoons vegetable shortening

1 teaspoon salt

1 cup dried blueberries, finely chopped

Oil for frying

Powdered sugar, for dusting

White Chocolate Sauce

1 (10-ounce) package white chocolate chips

1 1/4 cups heavy whipping cream

To make the beignets: Combine the water, 1 tablespoon sugar, and evaporated milk in a small saucepan, and heat over low heat until lukewarm, stirring to dissolve the sugar. Pour into a small bowl. Stir in the yeast. Let stand for 5 minutes. In a food processor with a steel blade, combine the flour, 1/3 cup sugar, egg, shortening, and salt. Turn processor off and on 3 or 4 times. Add the yeast mixture and repeat the process to incorporate. Process for 15 to 20 seconds to knead the dough.

Place the dough in a lightly oiled bowl, turning to coat all sides. Cover with plastic wrap. Let rise until doubled in bulk, about 1 1/2 hours. Punch down the dough, and add the blueberries. Turn out onto a lightly floured board. Roll to 1/2-inch thickness. Cut into 30 diamond-shaped 2 x 2-inch pieces. Place on an ungreased baking sheet. Cover loosely with plastic wrap. Let rise until doubled in bulk, about 45 minutes.

Heat the oil to 365 degrees in a deep fryer. Place the beignets in the hot oil a few at a time. Fry until golden brown, about 2 minutes per side. Remove and drain on paper towels. Sift with powdered sugar. Serve hot. Place 3 beignets on a serving plate, and ladle with the white chocolate sauce.

To make the sauce: Place the chocolate chips in the bowl of a double boiler over simmering water. Stir to melt until smooth. Remove from the heat, and stir in the heavy cream. Pour immediately over the beignets.

Makes 10 servings

PEACH-BLUEBERRY SMOOTHIE

A great breakfast drink.

1 1/2 cups fresh or frozen peach slices
1 cup ice cubes
1 cup plain yogurt
1 small banana, sliced
1/2 cup frozen blueberries
1/3 cup orange juice
3 tablespoons honey

Combine the peaches, ice cubes, yogurt, banana, blueberries, orange juice, and honey in a blender. Process until smooth. Serve immediately.

Makes 4 servings

CHOCOLATE-PECAN CRÈME BRÛLÉE

If you don't have a small torch, you should. You can get one at any hardware store.

Chocolate Layer

$1/2$ cup heavy whipping cream
1 tablespoon butter
1 tablespoon sugar
$3/4$ cup semi-sweet chocolate chips
$1/2$ cup pecans, toasted and chopped

Crème Brûlée

4 large egg yolks
$1/2$ cup sugar
$3/4$ cup milk
1 cup heavy whipping cream
1 teaspoon vanilla extract
$1/4$ cup sugar, topping for crème brûlée

To make the chocolate layer: Heat the cream, butter, and sugar together in a small saucepan over medium heat until the mixture comes to a boil. Place the chocolate chips in a small heat-resistant bowl. Pour the boiling cream mixture over the chocolate chips, stirring until the chocolate melts. Divide among eight $1/2$-cup ovenproof custard cups. Press 1 tablespoon of the pecans over each chocolate custard. Cover and refrigerate until the chocolate is firm, 6 hours or overnight.

To make the crème brûlée: In a medium bowl, whisk the egg yolks together with the sugar and set aside. In a small saucepan, bring the milk and cream to a boil. Temper $1/2$ cup of the hot mixture into the egg mixture. Pour the egg mixture into the hot milk, blending together. Add the vanilla. Cool completely.

Preheat the oven to 325 degrees. Divide the mixture evenly over the chocolate custard cups. Place the cups in a large baking pan. Pour hot water to come halfway up the side of the cups. Bake 45 to 50 minutes. Cool completely. Sprinkle 2 teaspoons sugar over each cup. Place under the broiler to caramelize the sugar or use a torch until the sugar melts and turns to a golden syrup. Serve cold.

Makes 8 servings

SOUTHERN GLAZED DOUGHNUTS

Cook these when you have a big crowd coming over. Otherwise, the temptation to eat more than you probably should is just too great.

Doughnuts
1 (13-ounce) can evaporated milk
$1/2$ cup butter
3 tablespoons sugar
1 teaspoon salt
1 package dry yeast
$1/4$ cup lukewarm water
4 cups all-purpose flour, divided
2 large egg yolks
Vegetable oil for frying

Glaze
3 cups powdered sugar
$1/4$ teaspoon salt
$1/2$ teaspoon vanilla extract
$1/2$ cup water
$1/4$ teaspoon cinnamon

To make the doughnuts: Heat the milk to the scalding point over medium heat in a small saucepan. Add the butter, sugar, and salt, stirring to dissolve. Remove from the heat and pour the mixture in a large bowl. Cool until it reaches a lukewarm temperature.

When the cooling period is complete, dissolve the yeast in water and let set for 5 minutes or until it bubbles. Add the yeast to the milk mixture and stir in 2 cups of flour. Cover and let rise for 1 hour. Stir, add the egg yolks and remaining flour, and continue to beat with a wooden spoon for 30 strokes. Cover and let rise for 1 hour. Punch down the dough and turn out onto a floured board. Roll to $1/2$-inch thickness. Cut with a 3-inch doughnut cutter. Cover with plastic wrap and let rise for 1 hour. Remove the plastic wrap.

Pour 3 inches of vegetable oil into a deep frying pan and bring the oil to 365 degrees. Fry the doughnuts a few at a time for 1 to 2 minutes per side or until golden brown. Remove and drain on paper towels. Glaze while hot.

To make the glaze: Mix the sugar, salt, vanilla, water, and cinnamon together in a large bowl. Dip the fried doughnuts in the glaze. Place on a serving tray and watch them disappear.

Makes 20 doughnuts

FIG MUFFINS

This recipe reminds me of one of the dearest women I have ever been lucky enough to know, Barbara Mayo. She is the mother of my equally dear niece Jan Carol. Barbara had fig trees in the front yard of her home in Georgia and was a master at using figs in her cooking.

$^{1}/_{2}$ cup butter, softened
$^{2}/_{3}$ cup sugar
2 large eggs
1 $^{1}/_{2}$ cups all-purpose flour
2 teaspoons baking powder
$^{1}/_{2}$ teaspoon cinnamon
$^{1}/_{4}$ teaspoon ground cloves
$^{1}/_{8}$ teaspoon salt
$^{1}/_{2}$ cup milk
$^{1}/_{2}$ cup fig preserves
$^{3}/_{4}$ cup chopped pecans

Preheat the oven to 350 degrees. Grease and flour two 12-cup muffin tins, or line with paper liners.

In a medium bowl, cream the butter and sugar together with an electric mixer until light and fluffy. Add the eggs, one at a time, beating well. In a small bowl, combine the flour, baking powder, cinnamon, cloves, and salt. Add to the creamed mixture alternately with the milk, stirring until moistened. Stir in the fig preserves and pecans. Spoon the batter into the muffin tins, filling $^{2}/_{3}$ full. Bake 20 minutes, or until a tester inserted in the middle of each muffin comes out clean. Serve warm.

Makes 24 muffins

SURPRISE COCONUT PIE

The surprise here is that this pie makes its own crust.

1 1/2 cups sugar
1/2 cup self-rising flour
4 large eggs, well beaten
2 cups milk
1/4 cup butter, melted
1 teaspoon vanilla extract
1/8 teaspoon salt
1 1/2 cups flaked coconut

Preheat the oven to 350 degrees. Grease a 10-inch pie plate.

In a small bowl, stir together the sugar and flour. Combine the eggs, milk, butter, vanilla, salt, and coconut in a large mixing bowl. Add the sugar mixture to the egg mixture. Pour into the prepared pie plate. Bake 45 minutes or until golden brown.

Makes 6 to 8 servings

Sweet Potato Muffins

These are delicious served with fresh fruit.

$1/2$ cup butter, softened
1 $1/4$ cups sugar
2 large eggs
1 $1/4$ cups mashed sweet potatoes
1 $1/2$ cups all-purpose flour
2 teaspoons baking powder
$1/4$ teaspoon salt
1 teaspoon cinnamon
1 cup milk
$3/4$ cup walnuts
$1/2$ cup raisins, chopped

Preheat the oven to 400 degrees. Grease two 12-cup muffin tins or line with paper liners.

In a small bowl, cream the butter and sugar with an electric mixer. Add the eggs, mixing well. Stir in the sweet potatoes. In a small bowl, sift together the flour, baking powder, salt, and cinnamon. Alternately add the dry mixture and the milk to the sweet potato mixture. Fold in the walnuts and raisins. Fill the prepared muffin tins $2/3$ full. Bake 25 minutes or until a tester inserted in the center of each muffin comes out clean.

Makes 24 muffins

Chapter 8

❧

WHEN NEIGHBORS
GIVE YOU LEMONS . . .

Brooke was proud of her husband, Trey, when he got a job at the Luckettville Savings and Loan right after he received his MBA. It meant relocating from their hometown about three hours away, but Brooke didn't care. Although she believed in women's liberation (to a degree), Brooke also believed in being a good wife. So she took it upon herself to get them settled in their new home. Trey had enough on his plate.

Brooke was a woman who knew what she wanted—she had zeroed in on Trey from across the room at a friend's wedding and declared him "the one" before having exchanged a word—and she knew she wanted the Craftsman bungalow the minute she stepped onto the front porch. She imagined her future children playing there before the realtor even told her the price, which barely registered with Brooke because she was too busy imagining the flower beds and wondering what color to repaint the shutters.

The closing went off without a hitch, as the seller's daughter was in a hurry to get her mother moved out to California.

"She was the best baker in town," whispered the realtor. "More than one person cried when they learned they'd never eat another slice of pie from Annabelle's Bakery."

Rumor had it someone was already snooping around to take over the bakery space, but the realtor hadn't been able to confirm that, so she kept her mouth shut.

After just a few days in their new home, Brooke has almost gotten the boxes unpacked in the living room when she hears a knock at the front door. She reminds herself to call an electrician to check the doorbell.

"Welcome to the neighborhood. I brought you a little something."

Brooke guesses the woman to be in her late fifties or early sixties, although she can't be sure because the woman is holding a cake plate in such a position as to partially obscure her face.

"It's a lemon layer cake," says the voice. "Do you like lemons?"

Just as she asks this question, Marian Prentiss realizes the lemon cake was a risk. She should have brought something more straightforward, like homemade blackberry jelly or devil's food brownies. But this cake is so good that she likes to share the family favorite whenever she can. That is just like Marian, though, who always means well, to get so excited that she didn't stop to think before she acted.

"Lemons are my favorite," replies Brooke, who had been taught not to say anything if it couldn't be nice. It just so happens that she does love both the fragrance and the taste of lemons, so she's not forced to tell a little white lie to this sweet woman who is the first person to welcome her to the neighborhood.

"I hear your husband is working at Luckettville Savings and Loan."

"Yes," says Brooke, a bit taken aback that the woman already knows something about her. She'd been warned about small towns, but she hadn't realized you were fair game once you hit the county line.

"And you are?"

"Marian," says the woman. "Marian Prentiss. Excuse my manners. I live just down the block, the old Tudor with the boxwoods out front.

"My Howard worked there," she continues, lowering the cake plate to her chest so that she and Brooke are looking at one another straight on.

"Started out part-time in college and worked his way up. Stayed until retirement."

Brooke doesn't know whether she needs to introduce herself or not. Seeing as how Marian already knows where her husband works, Brooke wonders what else might have already made the rounds about them. Does Marian know she has put on ten pounds since she and Trey married? Has word already gotten out that try as she might, Brooke can't find her way around the kitchen? Although Brooke has inherited her mother's good looks, and her preference for the underdog, she missed out on the cooking gene.

She's learned to make a decent pot roast, and she can do things to chicken with

a bottle of Italian dressing that most women wouldn't dream of. But it is dessert that stymies her, as she has never been able to combine sugar and butter without everything clumping up. The first time she cooked for Trey, back when they were dating, she had to rely on a store-bought pie that was still frozen in the center when she tried to cut it. They ended up eating around the edges, using their forks to break off little bites as the pie thawed. Trey was nice about it, like always. His ability to soothe her insecurities is one of the reasons Brooke married him.

But baking still gives her pause. She escorts Marian Prentiss into her home, apologizing for the mess, and thanks her for the cake.

"The family next door to you, on the corner, has been here for about five years. But they don't socialize much," said Marian. "Every summer I invite the whole neighborhood over for homemade ice cream, but they never come. Not so much as a thank-you for being invited.

"And on the other side, well, let's just say we're not sure if they're married or not."

Before Brooke can get a word in, Marian announces that she is sorry, but she has to go. Her bridge club is having its last gathering of the year, and she wants to get there before the punch runs out.

BLACKBERRY CRUMB PIE

There is nothing harder to pick than wild blackberries. Regardless whether you make this pie with berries you pick yourself in the hot summer sun or from ones you buy in the store, you are going to love this pie. This has been a staple of my cooking classes for years.

Filling

1 1/2 cups blackberries
1 (9-inch) pie shell, unbaked
2 large eggs
1 1/2 cups sugar
1/3 cup all-purpose flour
1/2 cup evaporated milk

Topping

1/4 cup butter
1/2 cup all-purpose flour
1/2 cup sugar
1/8 teaspoon salt

To make the filling: Preheat the oven to 325 degrees. Put the blackberries in the pie shell. In a small bowl, mix together the eggs, sugar, flour, and evaporated milk. Pour the mixture over the blackberries.

To make the topping: In a small bowl, mix the butter, flour, sugar, and salt until the mixture becomes crumbly. Sprinkle over the top of the filling. Bake 50 to 55 minutes, or until the top is golden brown.

Makes 6 to 8 servings

Homemade Blackberry Jelly

If it's not a sin not to make a pan of homemade biscuits to enjoy this jelly with, it sure should be.

1 gallon ripe blackberries, washed
4 1/2 cups sugar

Cook the blackberries in a large stockpot. Do not add water. The only water needed is what hangs to the berries after washing. Bring to a boil over high heat. Reduce the heat to medium and continue to cook for 10 minutes, stirring occasionally. Remove from the heat and pour the berries into a strainer, being careful not to mash them. This will equal approximately 3 cups of juice. Discard the berries.

Place 3 cups of the blackberry juice in a medium saucepan. Bring to a boil over medium-high heat. When the juice has begun a rolling boil, add the sugar, stirring constantly. Cook for 1 1/2 minutes or until jelly flakes off the spoon when held a few inches above the pan. Pour into sterilized pint jars. One cup of juice will yield 1 pint of jelly.

Makes 3 pints

orange chess pie

Chess pies are a Southern staple. I love the addition of the flavor of orange to this recipe.

1 1/2 cups sugar
1/2 cup butter, melted
4 large eggs, beaten
1 tablespoon cornmeal
1/4 teaspoon salt
1/3 cup orange juice
1 teaspoon grated orange zest
1 tablespoon lemon juice
1 (9-inch) pie shell, unbaked

Preheat the oven to 350 degrees. In a large bowl, cream together the sugar and butter. Whisk in the beaten eggs, cornmeal, salt, orange juice, orange zest, and lemon juice. Pour into the pie shell. Bake 45 minutes, or until a knife inserted in the center comes out clean. Cool before serving.

Makes 6 to 8 servings

PeCaN Pie WiTH HoNeY PeCaN ToPPiNG

I love honey. It gives this pecan pie a fresh and unique taste.

Pie
4 large eggs, slightly beaten
1 cup light corn syrup
1/4 cup sugar
1/4 cup brown sugar
3 tablespoons butter, melted
1 teaspoon vanilla extract
1/4 teaspoon salt
3/4 cup pecans, coarsely chopped
1 (9-inch) deep-dish pie shell, unbaked

Honey Topping
1/3 cup brown sugar, firmly packed
1/4 cup honey
1/4 cup butter
3/4 cups pecan halves

To make the pie: Preheat the oven to 350 degrees. Place the eggs in a medium mixing bowl. Add the corn syrup, sugar, brown sugar, butter, vanilla, and salt. Beat until mixed well. Add the chopped pecans. Pour into the pie shell and bake for 45 to 50 minutes. Remove the pie from the heat and spread the honey topping over the pie. Return the pie to the oven and cook for approximately 10 minutes or until the topping is golden brown. Cool slightly before slicing.

To make the topping: Combine the brown sugar, honey, and butter in a small saucepan. Cook over medium heat for 2 minutes or until the butter melts and the sugar dissolves, stirring constantly. Add the pecan halves and spread over the pie.

Makes 6 to 8 servings

DESSERT FOR THE ANGELS

This recipe is from my late sister-in-law, Mary Elizabeth Foster. She was one of the best cooks I have ever known.

1 angel food cake
$1/4$ cup cold water
2 (0.25 ounce) envelopes unflavored gelatin
1 cup boiling water
1 (20-ounce) can crushed pineapple, undrained
1 cup sugar
3 tablespoons lemon juice
$1/4$ teaspoon salt
1 (16-ounce) container frozen whipped topping, thawed
$1\,1/2$ cups toasted flaked coconut
Maraschino cherries (optional)

Break the angel food cake into small pieces and set aside. Put the cold water in a large bowl, and sprinkle the gelatin over the water. Let set for 1 minute. Stir in the boiling water until the gelatin is dissolved. Add the pineapple, sugar, lemon juice, and salt. Refrigerate until partially thickened, about 1 hour. Fold in the whipped topping. Place half the cake pieces in a 13 x 9-inch glass dish. Top with half the pineapple filling. Repeat the layers. Sprinkle with the toasted coconut, and garnish with the maraschino cherries.

Cover and refrigerate for 4 hours. Cut into squares and serve. Cover and refrigerate leftovers.

Makes 16 to 20 servings

DROP-BY COOKIES AND CREAM PIE

This is a great freezer pie. I keep one on hand all the time in case unexpected company stops by.

1 1/2 cups light whipping cream
1 (3-ounce) box vanilla instant pudding
1 (8-ounce) container frozen whipped topping, thawed
1 cup chocolate cream-filled cookies, slightly crushed
1 (9-inch) chocolate cookie pie crust

Pour the light cream into a medium mixing bowl. Add the vanilla pudding mix. Whisk for 1 minute. Let stand for 5 minutes. Fold in the whipped topping and cookies. Spoon the mixture into the pie crust. Cover and freeze until firm, about 6 hours or overnight. When ready to serve, remove from the freezer and let stand 10 minutes.

Makes 6 to 8 servings

CHOCOLATE GRAVY

This is a true Southern delicacy.

1/2 cup sugar
1 tablespoon all-purpose flour
1 tablespoon cocoa
1/8 teaspoon salt
1 cup milk
1 teaspoon vanilla extract
1 tablespoon butter

Stir together the sugar, flour, cocoa, and salt in a small saucepan. Add the milk and place over medium heat. Bring to a boil, stirring constantly, until the mixture thickens, about 2 minutes. Add the vanilla and butter. Serve hot over biscuits.

Makes 4 to 6 servings

TURTLE CHEESECAKE

This cheesecake should be made the day before you are going to serve it.

Crumb Crust

1 1/2 cups graham cracker crumbs

2 tablespoons sugar

1/4 cup butter, melted

Filling

1 (14-ounce) package caramels

2/3 cup evaporated milk

1 cup chopped pecans

2 (8-ounce) packages cream cheese, softened

2/3 cup sugar

1 teaspoon vanilla extract

2 large eggs

2/3 cup semi-sweet chocolate chips

Topping

1 cup sour cream

1/2 cup sugar

1/2 teaspoon vanilla extract

To make the crust: Preheat the oven to 350 degrees. Mix the graham cracker crumbs, sugar, and butter. Press over the bottom and 1 inch up the sides of a 9-inch springform pan. Bake 8 minutes.

To make the filling: Melt the caramels and evaporated milk together over low heat, stirring constantly. Spread over the baked crust. Sprinkle with the chopped pecans. Combine the cream cheese, sugar, and vanilla in a medium mixing bowl. Beat with an electric mixer until smooth. Add the eggs one at a time. Stir in the chocolate chips. Pour into the prepared pan. Bake 30 minutes. Remove and spread with the topping.

To make the topping: Stir together the sour cream, sugar, and vanilla in a small bowl. Spread over the cheesecake and return to the oven to cook for 10 minutes. Chill in the refrigerator. Remove from the springform pan to serve.

Makes 12 servings

CHERRY COFFEECAKE

This is a simple and delicious recipe.

2 cups all-purpose flour
1 teaspoon baking powder
1/2 teaspoon salt
3/4 cup plus 1/4 cup sugar, divided
1 cup vegetable oil
4 large eggs, slightly beaten
1 teaspoon vanilla extract
1 (20-ounce) can cherry pie filling
1 teaspoon cinnamon
1/2 cup pecans, chopped

Preheat the oven to 350 degrees. Grease and flour a 13 x 9-inch baking dish.

Sift the flour, baking powder, and salt in a medium mixing bowl. Add 3/4 cup sugar, oil, and eggs, stirring to mix well. Mix in the vanilla. Pour half the batter into the prepared pan. Cover with the pie filling. Top with the remaining batter.

In a small bowl, combine the remaining 1/4 cup of sugar, cinnamon, and pecans. Sprinkle over the batter. Bake 30 minutes or until a cake tester inserted in the center comes out clean. Cool slightly before serving.

Makes 16 servings

Lemon Layer Cake

Cake

2 ½ cups cake flour

½ teaspoon salt

2 ½ teaspoons baking powder

1 cup butter, softened

1 ¾ cup sugar

1 cup milk

5 large egg whites, stiffly beaten (save 2 yolks
    for the filling)

1 teaspoon lemon extract

Filling

¾ cup sugar

3 tablespoons cornstarch

½ cup water

½ cup orange juice

2 teaspoons lemon zest

3 tablespoons lemon juice

2 large egg yolks, slightly beaten

2 tablespoons butter

Lemon Cream Cheese Icing

1 (8-ounce) package cream cheese, softened

½ cup butter, softened

3 tablespoons lemon juice

2 teaspoons lemon zest

3 ½ to 4 cups powdered sugar

To make the cake: Preheat the oven to 350 degrees. Grease and flour three 8-inch cake pans.

In a medium bowl, sift the cake flour, salt, and baking powder together three times and set aside. In a large bowl, cream the butter and sugar together until fluffy. Alternately add the flour mixture and the milk to the creamed mixture, beginning and ending with the flour. Fold in the stiffly beaten egg whites and lemon extract. Divide the batter among the prepared cake pans. Bake 20 to 25 minutes. Cool in the pan for 10 minutes. Remove to a cake rack to cool.

To make the filling: Combine the sugar, cornstarch, water, orange juice, lemon zest, lemon juice, and egg yolks in a small saucepan. Cook over medium heat, stirring constantly, until the mixture comes to a boil. Boil 1 minute. Add the butter and cool completely.

To make the icing: Beat the cream cheese, butter, lemon juice, and lemon zest together until creamy. Beat in the powdered sugar, 1 cup at a time, adding additional sugar if necessary for spreading consistency.

To assemble: Place one layer on a cake plate. Spread with half the lemon filling. Top with the second cake layer, and spread with the remaining filling. Top with the third layer. Spread the cream cheese icing over the top and sides of the cake. Cover and refrigerate.

Makes 16 servings

HoNeY BuN Cake With VaNiLLa GLaZe

In the South, when someone dies, people bring food. This cake was brought to our home when my sweet mother-in-law, Flora, passed away. It is absolutely delicious. I asked my dear friend Margie Davis to share the recipe.

Cake

1 (18.25-ounce) yellow cake mix with pudding in the mix

1 large egg, slightly beaten

1/3 cup vegetable oil

1/3 cup water

1 cup sour cream

Filling

1/2 cup brown sugar, firmly packed

1 teaspoon cinnamon

1 cup pecans, chopped

Vanilla Glaze

1 cup powdered sugar

2 tablespoons milk

1/2 teaspoon vanilla extract

To make the cake: Preheat the oven to 350 degrees. Lightly grease and flour a 13 x 9-inch baking pan.

In a medium mixing bowl, combine the cake mix, egg, oil, water, and sour cream. Mix at medium speed with an electric mixer until smooth. Set aside.

To make the filling: Combine the brown sugar, cinnamon, and pecans in a small bowl.

To assemble: Pour half the batter into the prepared pan. Sprinkle half the brown sugar mixture over the batter. Top with the remaining cake batter and the remaining brown sugar mixture. Gently swirl with a knife. Bake 30 to 35 minutes or until a cake tester inserted in the center comes out clean.

To make the glaze: Mix the sugar, milk, and vanilla in a small bowl. Drizzle over the hot cake.

Makes 16 servings

GRANDCHILDREN'S FAVORITE BANANA CHOCOLATE CHIP MUFFINS

This recipe has long been a favorite of my grandchildren. Their mother (my daughter) always insisted that when there was a recipe they were really fond of, they learn to make it themselves too. Both grandchildren are in college now, and both can make these muffins from memory.

1/2 cup butter, softened
4 ounces cream cheese, softened
1 cup brown sugar, firmly packed
2 large ripe bananas, mashed
1 large egg, slightly beaten
1/4 cup sour cream
1 teaspoon vanilla extract
1 1/2 cups all-purpose flour
1 teaspoon baking soda
1 teaspoon baking powder
1/2 teaspoon salt
1 cup chocolate chips

Preheat the oven to 325 degrees. Lightly grease one 12-cup and one 6-cup muffin tin, or use paper liners.

In a small mixing bowl, cream together the butter, cream cheese, and brown sugar. Add the bananas, egg, sour cream, and vanilla, mixing well. In a large bowl, combine the flour, baking soda, baking powder, and salt. Add the banana mixture to the flour mixture, and mix well. Fold in the chocolate chips. Fill the muffin tins 2/3 full, and bake for 20 to 25 minutes or until a cake tester inserted in the center comes out clean and the muffins are golden brown.

Makes 18 muffins

DEVIL'S FOOD CREAM CHEESE BROWNIES

Appropriately titled, these are just sinfully good.

Brownies

1 cup chopped walnuts

2 tablespoons plus 1/2 cup melted butter, divided

1 teaspoon cinnamon

2 large eggs, slightly beaten

1 (18.25-ounce) devil's food cake mix

1 cup chocolate chips

Topping

2 large eggs, well beaten

1 (8-ounce) package of cream cheese, softened

1 pound powdered sugar (3 3/4 cups)

1 teaspoon vanilla extract

To make the brownies: Preheat the oven to 300 degrees. Lightly grease and flour a 13 x 9-inch baking pan.

Place the walnuts, 2 tablespoons butter, and cinnamon in a small saucepan over low heat, stirring until the butter is melted and the walnuts are toasted, 3 to 4 minutes. Let cool. Place the eggs in a medium mixing bowl. Add 1/2 cup melted butter, cake mix, and chocolate chips, stirring to mix well. Add the cooled cinnamon nut mixture. Press into the prepared pan and set aside while you prepare the topping.

To make the topping: Place the eggs, cream cheese, sugar, and vanilla in a medium mixing bowl. Using an electric mixer, mix at low speed for 1 minute, continuing to mix until the batter is smooth. Spread over the brownie mixture. Bake 45 minutes, or until the topping is lightly browned.

Makes 16 servings

peach preserves

These preserves are great on biscuits, of course, but try them on a ham sandwich. You will love it.

5 cups peaches, peeled and chopped
3 cups sugar
2 teaspoons lemon juice

Place the peaches in a large saucepan. Stir in the sugar and lemon juice. Stir and cook over medium-high heat for 25 minutes or until the syrup has thickened. While the peaches are cooking, sterilize the jars by placing 3 half-pint jars, rings, and tops in boiling water. Fill each hot jar with the cooked peach preserves, and cover with a hot lid and ring. Screw to tighten. The jars will seal as they cool.

Makes 3 half-pints

hot spiced tea mix

A great wintertime treat.

1 cup instant tea
1 1/2 cups sugar or sugar substitute
2 cups orange drink mix (Tang)
1 cup lemonade mix
1 teaspoon ground cloves
1 teaspoon ground cinnamon

Mix the tea, sugar, orange drink mix, lemonade mix, cloves, and cinnamon together. Store in a sealed container. To make 1 cup of tea, pour 1 cup boiling water over 3 teaspoons dry mix, stir, and serve hot.

Makes 64 servings

Chapter 9

❦

FAMILY REUNION

Jewel can't remember a summer when her entire extended family hasn't gathered for a reunion. Usually they meet at a state park in Kentucky or Tennessee because most everyone can get there without too much trouble. So she is surprised when so many Pattersons from across the region claim they are too busy to make time for a weekend of food and fellowship. The reunion has been their tradition since Jewel was a child, many moons ago. She guesses she should just be glad they got together at all, like Christmas and Easter, for some of her friends say they never see their relatives on a regular basis. But still, it bothers her that there won't be carloads of Pattersons making their way toward one another on a Saturday in July. There will be no grilling out, no badminton, no sharing of stories amongst the generations. No worrying about whether Mason will embarrass everyone with his jokes, so old they had whiskers.

Jewel reckons it just isn't meant to be. Junior has some sort of internship that keeps him working, even on Saturdays. His mama is getting her tummy tucked, and they haven't seen his daddy since he ran off around 1996. Ruby has to go to Happy Trails Retirement Village to sit with her mother, who has been complaining that no one ever comes to see her even though Ruby and her brother take turns dropping by several times a week. Lewis has to finish his community service, which he feels was unfairly imposed upon him by the judicial system but which the rest of the family considers a lucky break. Cousin Mason is manning a booth at the farmers' expo, and his wife, Crystal, has to drive the kids to a soccer tournament. Jewel doesn't understand why children today have to be involved in so many extracurricular activities, but no one asks for her opinion. When she was raising children, they considered themselves lucky to have county fairs and Vacation Bible School.

And so it goes, with each call that Jewel makes as she ticks her way through her address book. It seems that every last relative she talks to has some excuse or the other why he or she can't make it.

Jewel isn't one to give up easily; never has been. With the next few calls, her luck turns, ever so slightly, and she finds a handful of her kinfolk who want to meet, a smattering of souls who can't imagine not seeing one another. So they decide to put on a scaled-down version of their usual reunion. Jewel will host at her place because she has the biggest house. (The one time they tried to have the reunion at a restaurant had been a disaster. Jewel still hadn't had the nerve to show her face there after the scene Mason made when he was told they were out of Tabasco.) Everyone is assigned a dish, and thankfully the Pattersons who are planning to attend happen to be the best cooks of the bunch.

The more Jewel thinks about it, the more she wonders whether having fewer people might be a blessing in disguise. Jewel has always been one to look on the bright side. Hadn't she been the only one to cling to hope that time when Mother got sick with a mysterious illness and everyone gave up on her? Everyone except Jewel, that is, who wasn't surprised one bit when Mother got out of that hospital bed a week later, good as new, to live fifteen more years without developing so much as a fever.

So this year Jewel won't have to pretend to enjoy Cousin Samantha's three-bean salad when she can barely swallow a forkful. Too much vinegar. Nor will Jewel be expected to proclaim how talented the twins are when, in reality, she finds their need to hog the limelight something they should have grown out of by now. With a grateful heart, Jewel realizes she'll be spared the hour-long debate with Dudley about state politics. He always has been too liberal for her taste.

Instead, the remaining Pattersons decide to bring only their favorite foods to the reunion: cold spaghetti salad, oven-roasted beef tenderloin, and jalapeño bacon cornbread. As for desserts, they choose Bay's fudge pie, Verna's sour cream apple pie, Wilma's key lime pie, and banana pudding.

This time there won't be a ton of leftover coleslaw, which Aunt Marge insists is homemade even though they see her, year after year, dumping it out of big, plastic jars into bowls in the back of her station wagon. There will be no need to hide Sandra's brussels sprout soufflé under their napkins as they tell her yes, they most certainly did appreciate her commitment to five daily servings of vegetables.

So even though there won't be as many people as usual at the annual Patterson reunion—they will all fit around Jewel's dining room table once she puts the leaf in—there will be plenty of food and more than enough family.

DIVIDED SOUTH BANANA PUDDING

In the South, there are two types of banana pudding—cooked and uncooked. This is the old Southern variety with meringue. Variety is the spice of the South.

Pudding
1 cup sugar
3 tablespoons cornstarch
2 cups milk
$1/8$ teaspoon salt
3 large egg yolks (save the whites for the meringue)
1 tablespoon butter
1 teaspoon vanilla extract
1 (15-ounce) box vanilla wafers
4 large bananas, sliced

Meringue
3 large egg whites
$1/2$ teaspoon cream of tartar
6 tablespoons sugar

To make the pudding: Combine the sugar and cornstarch in a medium saucepan. Stir in the milk and salt. Whisk in the egg yolks. Cook over medium heat, stirring constantly, until the mixture comes to a boil. Cook for an additional 3 to 5 minutes, stirring until thickened. Add the butter and vanilla. Remove from the heat. Layer the bottom of a 2-quart baking dish with $1/3$ of the wafers, $1/3$ of the bananas, and $1/3$ of the cooked filling. Repeat 2 more times. Top with the meringue.

To make the meringue: Preheat the oven to 350 degrees. Beat the egg whites and cream of tartar together in the bowl of an electric mixer until soft peaks form. Gradually add the sugar. Continue to beat until stiff peaks form. Spread over the banana pudding. Bake 8 to 10 minutes. Serve warm or cold.

Makes 6 to 8 servings

ZUCCHINI BREAD

Southerners love growing zucchini. This bread is delicious and easy to make.

3 cups all-purpose flour
2 teaspoons baking soda
1 teaspoon salt
1/2 teaspoon baking powder
2 teaspoons cinnamon
1 cup chopped pecans
3 large eggs
2 cups sugar
1 cup vegetable oil
2 teaspoons vanilla extract
2 cups zucchini, unpeeled and shredded (about 1 medium)
1 (8-ounce) can crushed pineapple, well drained

Preheat the oven to 325 degrees. Grease and flour two 9 x 5 x 3-inch loaf pans.

Combine the flour, baking soda, salt, baking powder, cinnamon, and pecans in a large bowl. Set aside. Beat the eggs in a large mixing bowl. Add the sugar, oil, and vanilla. Mix until creamy. Add the zucchini and crushed pineapple. Add the flour mixture. Stir only until all ingredients are moistened. Divide the batter between the loaf pans.

Bake 1 1/2 hours, or until a toothpick inserted in the middle of the pan comes out clean. Cool 10 minutes before removing from the pans. Cool completely before slicing. This bread freezes well.

Makes 2 loaves

PEANUT BUTTER SAUCE

Serve with vanilla or chocolate ice cream.

1 cup sugar
1 tablespoon light corn syrup
3/4 cup light whipping cream
1/3 cup peanut butter
1 teaspoon vanilla extract

Mix the sugar, syrup, and cream together in a medium saucepan. Bring to a boil over medium heat. Cook for 5 minutes, stirring constantly. Remove from the heat, and stir in the peanut butter and vanilla. Let cool. Store in a covered container in the refrigerator.

Makes 8 to 10 servings

MARSHMALLOW ICE CREAM

Thanks to my friend Luanne Greer, this has become my new go-to ice cream recipe. No eggs, no cooking, no mixer. Just stir and freeze. And it also makes a great base for any fruits or candies you want to add.

1 (13-ounce) jar marshmallow cream
1 (14-ounce) can condensed milk
1 pint heavy whipping cream
1/2 gallon milk
1 (16-ounce) can chocolate syrup (optional)

In a large mixing bowl, combine the marshmallow cream, condensed milk, and cream. Mix until smooth. Whisk in the milk. Pour into an ice cream freezer, and freeze according to the manufacturer's directions. Stir in the chocolate syrup and serve.

Makes 1 gallon

CONCORD GRAPE PIE

Concord grapes are a fall fruit, but it's worth the wait. This pie is delicious.

3 1/2 cups Concord grapes, washed and stemmed
1 cup sugar
1/4 cup all-purpose flour
1/8 teaspoon salt
2 tablespoons butter, melted
1 tablespoon lemon juice
2 (9-inch) pie crusts, unbaked

Preheat the oven to 350 degrees. Pinch the grapes to separate the skins from the pulp. Save the skins. Place the pulp in a medium saucepan and cook over medium heat, stirring constantly for 3 to 5 minutes. While the pulp is hot, press through a sieve to remove the seeds.

Combine the sugar, flour, and salt in a medium mixing bowl. Stir in the grape skins, cooked pulp, butter, and lemon juice. Pour into the pie shell. Cover with the additional pie crust. Cut 3 to 4 slits for the steam to escape. Bake 40 to 45 minutes, or until the crust is golden brown. It is best to let cool completely before serving.

Makes 6 to 8 servings

WILMA'S KEY LIME PIE

My sister-in-law Wilma Foster is such a gracious hostess. It is always a treat to be invited to her home.

1 (9-inch) graham cracker crust (see recipe on page 8)
3 large egg yolks at room temperature
1 teaspoon lime zest, grated (2 key limes)
1 (14-ounce) can sweetened condensed milk
2/3 cup fresh key lime juice
1 cup heavy whipping cream
1 tablespoon powdered sugar
1 key lime, thinly sliced for garnish

Preheat the oven to 350 degrees. Bake the graham cracker crust and let cool.

In a medium mixing bowl, beat the egg yolks and lime zest together with an electric mixer at medium speed until fluffy, about 5 minutes. Gradually add the condensed milk, and continue to beat until the mixture is thick, about 4 minutes. Slowly add the lime juice, beating at low speed, mixing until just combined. Pour the filling into the pie shell. Bake 10 minutes, or until the pie is set. Cool completely, then refrigerate for 2 hours. Freeze for at least 20 minutes.

Whip the heavy cream and powdered sugar together in a small bowl until stiff. Cover and place in the refrigerator until ready to serve. To serve, spread whipped cream over the pie and garnish with thinly sliced limes.

This pie may be covered and frozen for a month. If frozen, remove from the freezer 20 minutes before serving.

Makes 6 to 8 servings

CHOCOLATE SAUCE

This is heaven over homemade vanilla ice cream.

1 cup semi-sweet chocolate chips
1 cup heavy whipping cream
$1/4$ cup sugar
1 tablespoon butter
1 tablespoon light corn syrup
$1/2$ teaspoon vanilla extract

Place the chocolate chips in a medium bowl and set aside. In a small saucepan over medium heat, bring the cream, sugar, butter, and corn syrup to a boil. Pour the mixture over the chocolate chips. Add the vanilla. Cover and let sit 5 to 8 minutes. Whisk until the mixture is smooth. The sauce will keep in the refrigerator for up to 10 days. Serve over ice cream.

Makes 1 $1/2$ cups

CHOCOLATE CHIP PECAN PIE

This is my daughter's recipe. We all love her, but we're not sure we would love her quite as much if she didn't bring this with her whenever our family gets together to enjoy a meal.

$1/2$ cup butter, melted and cooled
1 cup sugar
$1/2$ cup self-rising flour
2 large eggs, slightly beaten
1 teaspoon vanilla extract
$3/4$ cup chocolate chips
1 cup pecans, chopped
1 (9-inch) pie shell, unbaked

Preheat the oven to 350 degrees. In a medium mixing bowl, cream together the butter, sugar, and flour. Add the eggs and vanilla. Stir in the chocolate chips and pecans. Pour the mixture into the pie crust. Bake 30 minutes or until golden brown.

Makes 6 to 8 servings

BROWN SUGAR ICE CREAM

I love the flavor of brown sugar. This sure does taste good on a hot summer day.

4 large eggs, beaten
1 pound dark brown sugar
2 tablespoons cornstarch
$1/8$ teaspoon salt
1 quart milk
1 quart light whipping cream
2 cups heavy whipping cream
1 teaspoon vanilla extract
1 cup toasted pecans, chopped

Place the eggs, sugar, cornstarch, salt, and milk in a heavy 2-quart saucepan. Cook over medium heat until the mixture comes to a boil, stirring constantly. Remove from the heat and let cool.

Add the creams, vanilla, and pecans to the cooled mixture. Pour the mixture into a 1-gallon ice cream freezer. Freeze according to the manufacturer's directions.

Makes 16 servings

Verna's Sour Cream Apple Pie with Cinnamon Topping

My sister-in-law Verna is a wonderful cook. I think you will enjoy her recipe for this apple pie.

Pie
2 tablespoons all-purpose flour
1/8 teaspoon salt
1 cup sugar
1 large egg
1 cup sour cream
1 teaspoon vanilla extract
1/2 teaspoon cinnamon
2 large tart apples, peeled and diced (about 2 cups)
1 (9-inch) pie crust, unbaked

Topping
1/3 cup sugar
1/3 cup all-purpose flour
1 teaspoon cinnamon
1/4 cup cold butter

To make the pie: Preheat the oven to 400 degrees. Sift the flour, salt, and sugar together. Using an electric mixer, beat in the egg, sour cream, vanilla, and cinnamon into the flour mixture. Continue to beat for about 2 minutes. Fold in the apples. Spoon the mixture into the crust, and bake about 10 minutes. Reduce the temperature to 350 degrees. Continue to bake for 30 minutes.

To make the topping: Combine the sugar, flour, cinnamon, and butter until it forms a crumbly mix. Remove the pie from the oven and sprinkle with the topping. Cook for an additional 15 minutes or until golden brown.

Makes 6 to 8 servings

WATERMELON POPSICLES

Just as refreshing as a slice of watermelon on a hot summer day.

4 cups watermelon, cubed
3 tablespoons sugar
1 tablespoon lemon juice
1/4 teaspoon salt

Place the watermelon, sugar, lemon juice, and salt in a blender. Blend at high speed until the mixture is pureed. Pour into twelve 3-ounce popsicle molds or 2 ice cube trays. When the popsicles begin to freeze, insert a wooden stick in each one. Cover, and freeze overnight.

Makes 12 servings

Note: You can also use paper cups for the molds.

Bay's Fudge Pie

At the time I am writing this book, my sister Elizabeth (Bay) is ninety-six years old. I don't know anyone who has cooked more or taken food to more people in need than she has. I know there are hundreds, if not thousands, of people who have been lucky enough to enjoy this delicious pie.

1/2 cup butter, melted and cooled
1 cup sugar
1/4 cup self-rising flour
1/4 cup cocoa
2 large eggs, beaten
1 teaspoon vanilla extract
1 (9-inch) pie shell, unbaked

Preheat the oven to 350 degrees. In a medium bowl, mix together the butter, sugar, flour, cocoa, eggs, and vanilla , stirring well to combine. Pour the mixture into the pie shell, and bake 25 to 30 minutes or until the pie is set.

Makes 6 to 8 servings

GERALDINE'S PAPER BAG APPLE PIE

My late sister-in-law from Louisville, Kentucky, was a great cook. Her death notice made mention of her always bringing desserts to the medical staff whenever she had a doctor's appointment. Her daughter Tammy said this was one of her most popular treats.

Pie

8 medium granny smith apples, peeled and
    sliced
2 1/2 tablespoons lemon juice
3/4 cup sugar
3 tablespoons all-purpose flour
1/2 teaspoon nutmeg
1/2 teaspoon cinnamon

1 teaspoon apple pie spice
1 (9-inch) pie crust, unbaked
1 large brown bag (grocery store type)

Topping

2/3 cup sugar
2/3 cup all-purpose flour
3/4 cup butter, frozen and sliced

To make the pie: Preheat the oven to 425 degrees. Mix the peeled and sliced apples with lemon juice in a large bowl and set aside. In a small bowl, mix together the sugar, flour, nutmeg, cinnamon, and apple pie spice. Sprinkle over the apples, tossing to mix well. Place the apple mix in the pie crust.

To make the topping: Mix the sugar and flour together. Mix the butter in with your fingers or a pastry blender until the mix resembles small peas. Sprinkle over the pie filling.

Slide the pie into a bag large enough to cover the pie loosely. Fold the end of the bag twice and clip closed with 4 paper clips. Bake 1 hour. Cut the bag open to cool.

Makes 6 to 8 servings

Note: Use this recipe only with an electric oven.

Chapter 10

❧

MARY BETH HAS A BRIDAL SHOWER

It had been so long since Mary Beth Fuller had even allowed herself to dream of marriage that by the time her soulmate came along, when she was nearing forty, she was shocked. Stunned, even. Having given up on the idea of ever finding Mr. Right, or even Mr. Good Companion, Mary Beth had thrown out all her dog-eared copies of bride magazines and wedding planners. She had canceled her online dating membership and stopped accepting blind dates with her friends' coworkers. When she went to the gym, it was to work out, not to scan the weight room for potential mates. She'd even started allowing herself to run to the Piggly Wiggly without her makeup on.

"You never know when you might meet someone," her mother used to say. "Try to look nice at all times. And be sweet."

It wasn't long after her own mother had given up that Madison came into Mary Beth's life.

Mary Beth is nothing if not practical, and she had, for all intents and purposes, accepted the reality that she would never in her life walk down the aisle as more than a nervous choirgirl or a taffeta-clad bridesmaid. So when Madison asked her to marry him, she hadn't a clue what was expected of a middle-aged bride. And although Mary Beth was over the moon for the man who was becoming her husband, she wondered whether making a fuss at their age—Madison was pushing fifty himself—was a bit unseemly.

If she was honest with herself, though, Mary Beth wouldn't mind wearing a beautiful dress and being the center of attention for just a brief time. Hasn't she waited long enough? Some of her friends are already on their third marriages, and Mary Beth hasn't even had a shot at one. Nor would she mind a few gifts, maybe a new blender or some such. For even though Mary Beth has been keeping house by herself for years and had, in fact, at age twenty-six hauled off and bought several place settings of Spode, she has to admit her cupboards and countertops were pretty bare. Cooking for one isn't all that appealing, so Mary Beth ate out a lot. Now, though, she wants that to change, so she and Madison can cook and eat their meals as a couple.

When several of her girlfriends offered to throw her a shower, she was delighted, even though one of the women seemed disappointed when Mary Beth said no to the suggestion of a lingerie theme.

Mary Beth's skinny days have long passed, if they'd ever existed, and the thought of people buying her large unmentionables was simply more than she could stand. So kitchen it was, and Mary Beth was delighted to get a fancy coffee maker with a built-in bean grinder and her first food processor. A gal could get used to such largesse.

There were also steak knives, kitchen towels, and cutting boards (one wood, another plastic). She opened a box of fabulous cookware with heat-resistant handles, and received cookbooks of all varieties. But to Mary Beth's mind, and heart, the best present of all was the collection of recipes put together for her by the guests. Each person brought an index card containing a treasured recipe from her own family to share with Mary Beth. Not only that, but they also brought samples of the foods and shared stories from their own family folklore to go with each one. Isn't that usually the way, that our favorite foods include not only instructions and ingredients but also memory and meaning?

Mary Beth's not sure where to start; the strawberry ice cream pie from Melissa was decadent and rich. Sandra's coconut banana bread made Mary Beth want to run home and whip up a loaf herself. As for Claudia's white chocolate brownies, the first taste took Mary Beth right back to the kitchen table of her childhood, when her mother first taught her not to put the big wooden spoon back in the batter after she had licked it.

In the years to come, Mary Beth will try every one of those recipes, tweaking them here and there as she becomes more confident in the kitchen. She will add several recipes from her own heritage to the collection so that she will be able to pass them down to her nieces when the time comes.

As for her wedding day, Mary Beth got even more than she'd allowed herself to imagine possible: an intimate ceremony in the same church where her parents were married in 1948, the blessing of having her oldest and dearest friends in attendance, and that delightful applause after she and her husband repeated their vows. Mary Beth had let go of any misgivings she'd had about being the center of attention and allowed herself to be honored by the people who matter to her most in the world.

For the rest of her years, the memory of that Saturday morning in April will feel like a blessing to her, like love.

caramel Pecan chocolate cake

The only thing better than this cake is this cake with a cold glass of milk.

1 (18.25-ounce) box German chocolate cake mix
1 (14-ounce) bag caramels
1/2 cup butter
1 (14-ounce) can condensed milk
1 1/2 cups milk chocolate chips, divided
1 cup pecans, chopped

Preheat the oven to 350 degrees. Grease and flour a 13 x 9-inch baking pan.

Prepare the cake mix as directed on the box. Pour half the batter into the pan, and bake 15 minutes. In a microwaveable bowl, melt the caramels, butter, and condensed milk, stirring often.

Remove the chocolate cake from the oven. Immediately pour half the caramel mixture over the cake. Sprinkle with 1 cup of the chocolate chips. Pour the remaining batter over the caramel layer. Bake 15 to 18 minutes. Cool slightly. Add the remaining 1/2 cup chocolate chips to the caramel, and spread on top of the cooled cake. Sprinkle with the chopped pecans.

Makes 12 to 16 servings

MaRie's Peach DesseRt

Last year I was injured on vacation, which left me out of commission for a while. I was so lucky to have some good friends stop by with sweets to cheer me up. This was one of my favorites, from my good friend Marie Wallace.

2 cups all-purpose flour
1 cup butter, melted
1 cup pecans, chopped
2 (8-ounce) packages cream cheese, softened
4 cups powdered sugar
8 medium peaches, peeled and sliced (reserve 7 slices for garnish)
1 (16-ounce) carton frozen whipped topping, thawed

Preheat the oven to 350 degrees. In a medium bowl, mix together the flour, butter, and chopped pecans. Press the mixture into a 13 x 9-inch baking dish. Bake 15 to 20 minutes or until lightly browned. Cool completely (this can be done the day before).

In a medium bowl, mix the cream cheese and powdered sugar together until smooth. Spread over the cooled crust. Cover with the peach slices. Spread with the thawed whipped topping. Garnish with the reserved peach slices. Cover and chill 1 hour before serving.

Makes 12 to 16 servings

WHITE CHOCOLATE BROWNIES

A lunchtime treat that will put a smile on anyone's face.

1 cup butter
1 (11-ounce) package plus 1/2 cup white chocolate chips, divided
1 cup sugar
2 teaspoons vanilla extract
4 large eggs, slightly beaten
2 cups all-purpose flour
1 cup walnuts, chopped

Preheat the oven to 325 degrees. Lightly grease and flour a 13 x 9-inch pan.

Slice the butter into tablespoons and place in the top of a double boiler over simmering water. Add the 11-ounce package of white chocolate chips, stirring over low heat until the mixture is smooth. Remove the double boiler from over the water, and add the sugar, vanilla, and eggs, stirring to mix well. Add the flour and walnuts, stirring to just combine. Pour the batter into the prepared pan. Bake 25 to 30 minutes, or until a cake tester inserted in the center comes out clean.

While the brownies are hot, top with the remaining 1/2 cup white chocolate chips and allow them to melt. Spread to cover the top. Cool.

Makes 12 to 16 servings

Peach Tea

If fresh peaches aren't in season when you are serving this, use mint.

1 (2-quart) package peach tea mix
4 cups water
1 cup apple juice
1 cup white grape juice
2 cups ginger ale
1/4 teaspoon almond extract
1 small fresh peach, cut in slices for garnish

Mix the tea together with the water in a large pitcher. Add the apple juice, grape juice, ginger ale, and almond extract. Stir to blend. Pour the tea into glasses full of ice, and garnish each glass with a peach slice.

Makes 8 servings

Emily's Chocolate Cream Toes

This recipe was given to me by my great-niece Emily Green. She has been lucky enough to learn how to cook from her grandmother, my sister Louise.

1 (16.6-ounce) package chocolate cream-filled cookies
1 (8-ounce) package cream cheese, softened
1 (16-ounce) package chocolate candy coating
Pink candy sprinkles

Crush the chocolate cookies in a food processor until fine crumbs are formed. Place the crumbs in a large mixing bowl. Add the cream cheese. Mix until well combined. Roll into small balls and place on waxed paper. Freeze for 2 hours.

Melt the chocolate coating in a double boiler over simmering water, stirring occasionally. Dip the balls in the coating mix, turning with 2 forks. Roll in candy sprinkles. Place on waxed paper and return to the freezer for a few hours or overnight. Serve at room temperature.

Makes 40 to 50 balls

CINNAMON CREAM BISCUITS WITH PECAN TOPPING

I love cinnamon rolls, but they do take a lot of time to make from scratch. These are quick, easy, and delicious.

Biscuits

1 cup heavy whipping cream

1 1/2 cups all-purpose flour, plus extra for dusting

4 teaspoons baking powder

1/2 teaspoon salt

2 tablespoons butter, melted

1/2 cup brown sugar, firmly packed

1 1/2 tablespoons cinnamon

Pecan Topping

3/4 cup brown sugar, firmly packed

3 tablespoons heavy whipping cream

3/4 cup pecans, finely chopped

1 teaspoon vanilla extract

To make the biscuits: Preheat the oven to 425 degrees. Lightly grease an 8-inch baking pan.

In a medium mixing bowl, whip the cream with an electric mixer on high speed until soft peaks form. In a small bowl, mix the flour, baking powder, and salt. Add the flour mixture to the whipped cream, stirring with a spatula, to form a stiff dough. Turn the dough out onto a lightly floured board and knead for about 1 minute.

Roll into a 12 x 9-inch rectangle, 1/4-inch thick. Brush with melted butter and sprinkle evenly with the brown sugar and cinnamon. Roll up from the long end to enclose the brown sugar mixture, pinching the seams together. Cut into 1-inch slices. Place the biscuits flat side down and close together in the prepared pan. Bake 12 to 15 minutes or until golden brown. While the biscuits are baking, prepare the topping.

To make the topping: Combine the brown sugar, cream, pecans, and vanilla in a small bowl. When the biscuits are done, spread the topping over the cinnamon biscuits and return them to the oven for an additional 4 minutes or until the topping is bubbly.

Makes 12 biscuits

Raspberry, Almond, and White Chocolate Coffeecake

This is a delicious breakfast or morning cake.

Cake

2 cups fresh raspberries

1/2 cup brown sugar

1 1/2 cups all-purpose flour

3/4 cups sugar

2 teaspoons baking powder

1/4 teaspoon salt

1/4 cup butter, softened

1/2 cup light whipping cream

1 large egg

1/2 cup white chocolate chips, divided

Streusel Topping

1/2 cup brown sugar

1/3 cup all-purpose flour

1/4 cup butter

1/2 cup sliced almonds

Glaze

1/2 cup powdered sugar

2 teaspoons milk

To make the cake: Preheat the oven to 350 degrees. Grease and flour a 9-inch springform pan.

In a small bowl, mix the raspberries and brown sugar. Set aside. In a medium mixing bowl, beat the flour, sugar, baking powder, salt, butter, cream, and egg together until just moistened with an electric mixer on medium speed. Spread half the batter in the bottom of the prepared pan. Sprinkle with half the raspberry mixture and 1/4 cup of the white chocolate chips. Layer the remaining batter, raspberries, and chocolate chips.

To make the topping: In a small bowl, mix the brown sugar, flour, butter, and almonds until it becomes a crumbly mixture. Top the batter with the streusel mixture. Bake 1 hour until golden brown, or until a cake tester inserted in the center comes out clean. Spread with the glaze.

To make the glaze: Combine the sugar and milk in a small bowl. Spread over the cake and serve.

Makes 8 servings

JUST PERFECT CHERRY WALNUT BARS WITH CHERRY ICING

Perfect for any bridge club or ladies lunch.

Pastry

1 cup all-purpose flour
1/2 cup butter
1/4 cup powdered sugar

Filling

2 large eggs, slightly beaten
1 cup sugar
1/4 cup all-purpose flour
2 teaspoons baking powder
1/4 teaspoon salt

1 teaspoon vanilla extract
1 cup walnuts, chopped
1/2 cup flaked coconut
1/2 cup maraschino cherries, halved (save the juice for the icing)

Cherry Icing

1/4 cup butter, softened
2 cups powdered sugar
4 tablespoons reserved cherry juice
4 tablespoons flaked coconut

To make the pastry: Preheat the oven to 350 degrees. In a small bowl, mix the flour, butter, and powdered sugar to create a crumbly mixture. Pat into a 12 x 9-inch baking pan. Bake 15 minutes.

To make the filling: In a small bowl, mix together the eggs, sugar, flour, baking powder, salt, vanilla, walnuts, coconut, and cherries until well combined. Spread over the baked crust. Bake 20 minutes, or until a cake tester inserted in the center comes out clean and the bars are golden brown. Cool. Frost with the cherry icing.

To make the icing: In a small bowl, combine the butter, powdered sugar, and cherry juice. Beat until smooth. Spread the icing over the cooled bars, and sprinkle with the coconut. Cut into bars and keep covered.

Makes 16 servings

APRICOT DIP

In addition to being a wonderful dip, this also tastes great on any fruit bread you bake.

1 (8-ounce) container sour cream
3/4 cup apricot preserves
2/3 cup flaked coconut
1/2 cup chopped walnuts
1/8 teaspoon salt
1 cantaloupe
1 honeydew

Mix the sour cream, apricot preserves, coconut, walnuts, and salt together in a small mixing bowl. Stir until smooth. Chill for 1 hour prior to serving.

Wash each melon and cut in half. Remove the seeds. Using a melon baller, press firmly into the flesh, turning clockwise, and pull the ball out of the melon. Cover and refrigerate the melon balls until ready to serve with the dip. Use toothpicks to dip the melon balls into the dip.

Makes 12 servings

OATMEAL CAKE WITH PECAN-COCONUT TOPPING

When my children were very young, we lived next door to Mrs. Eva Baker. And let me tell you, her name was appropriate: She sure could bake. This is just one of her recipes I am still making fifty years later.

Cake
1 cup oats
1 1/4 cups boiling water
1/2 cup butter, softened
1 cup sugar
1 cup brown sugar
2 large eggs, well beaten
1 teaspoon vanilla extract
1 1/3 cups all-purpose flour
1 teaspoon baking soda
1/2 teaspoon salt
1 teaspoon cinnamon

Topping
1 cup brown sugar
1/4 cup butter
1/2 cup evaporated milk
1 cup pecans, chopped
1 cup flaked coconut

To make the cake: Preheat the oven to 350 degrees. Grease a 13 x 9-inch baking pan.

Place the oats in a small bowl. Pour the boiling water over the oats and let stand for 20 minutes. In a large bowl, cream together the butter, sugar, and brown sugar with an electric mixer. Add the oats, beaten eggs, and vanilla. In a small bowl, sift together the flour, baking soda, salt, and cinnamon. Add to the cream mixture, beating only until well mixed. Pour into the prepared pan. Bake 30 to 35 minutes, or until a cake tester inserted in the center comes out clean.

To make the topping: Mix the brown sugar, butter, evaporated milk, pecans, and coconut together in a small saucepan. Bring to a boil over medium heat, stirring constantly. Boil 3 minutes. Spread over the warm cake.

Makes 16 servings

CHOCOLATE FONDUE

1 (11-ounce) package semi-sweet chocolate chips (2 cups)
1 (14-ounce) can condensed milk
1 (7-ounce) jar marshmallow cream
1/2 cup light whipping cream
1 teaspoon vanilla extract
Assorted fruits and pound cake for dipping

Combine the chocolate chips, condensed milk, marshmallow cream, whipping cream, and vanilla in the top of a double boiler over medium heat, stirring constantly to melt the chocolate. Place in the fondue pot to keep warm.

Good options for dipping:

Mandarin orange sections
Apple wedges
Strawberries
Bananas
Pineapple spears
Angel food cake pieces
Marshmallows

Makes 16 servings

Note: Use white chocolate chips to create a white chocolate fondue.

MINT TEA

I grow my own mint and love using it in this crowd-pleasing tea.

7 cups water, divided
4 regular-size tea bags
10 fresh mint sprigs
1/2 cup fresh lemon juice
1/2 cup fresh orange juice
1 1/4 cups sugar

Pour 4 cups water into a medium saucepan, and bring to a boil over high heat. Remove the pan from the heat and add the tea bags and mint. Cover to steep for 10 minutes. Remove the tea bags and mint, squeezing to extract flavor. Discard. Pour the tea into a 2-quart container. Add the lemon and orange juices, sugar, and 3 cups water. Chill and serve over ice.

Makes 4 to 6 servings

CHOCOLATE MARSHMALLOW SQUARES

These will remind you of Tennessee's most famous candy bar.

2 tablespoons butter
1 (11-ounce) package semi-sweet chocolate chips
1 (14-ounce) can sweetened condensed milk
2 cups roasted peanuts
1 (10-ounce) package miniature marshmallows

Butter a 13 x 9-inch glass dish. In the top of a double boiler, combine the butter, chocolate chips, and condensed milk, stirring until melted and smooth. Remove the double boiler from over the water. Stir in the peanuts and marshmallows. Spread the mixture into the buttered dish. Chill until firm. Cut into small squares and serve. Store leftovers covered at room temperature.

Makes 36 pieces

EMPTY-NESTER COCONUT BANANA NUT BREAD

One of my greatest failings as a parent is that neither of my children likes coconut. Now that they are grown and on their own, I can make things like this bread anytime I want.

1/2 cup shortening
1 cup sugar
2 large eggs
1 1/2 cups all-purpose flour
1 teaspoon baking soda
1/2 teaspoon salt
1 teaspoon vanilla extract
1 1/4 cups bananas, mashed (3 medium)
1/2 cup flaked coconut
1/2 cup pecans, chopped

Preheat the oven to 350 degrees. Grease and flour a 9 x 5-inch loaf pan.

In a large bowl, cream the shortening and sugar together with an electric mixer on medium speed for 2 minutes. Beat in the eggs, flour, baking soda, salt, and vanilla. Mix well. Stir in the bananas, coconut, and pecans. Pour the mixture into the prepared pan. Bake 1 hour, or until a cake tester inserted in the center comes out clean. Cool for 10 minutes in the pan before turning out onto a wire rack to cool completely.

Makes 12 servings

Chapter 11

HoLiDays AnD TRaDiTiOnS

The holidays were going to be big this year for the Tanner family. Al Junior would be home on leave from his stint in the army. He said he was bringing a girl, which made Big Al and Martha Lee Tanner somewhat uncomfortable, as their son's last girlfriend had turned out to be from Up East. Cute enough, to be sure, but not refined or traditional in a manner befitting the Tanners. They wanted their son to be happy, of course, so they had acted as if she were lovely. But they were secretly delighted when Al Junior phoned two weeks later to say the girl had dumped him in order to join the Peace Corps. Big Al and Martha Lee were hoping for the best this time around.

"I don't want to shock you," said Al Junior on the phone, "but she's a vegetarian."

For several seconds, Martha Lee was confused, thinking Junior was trying to tell her something about his girlfriend's politics.

"You'll need to pick up some tofu when you go to the grocery store," he continued, and that's when Martha Lee realized what was what. She had no idea which section of the A&P housed tofu, but she assured her son she'd take care of it.

The biggest news in the Tanner family, though, was that Ella, the oldest, was bringing her new baby. It seemed like nothing short of a miracle that the adoption had come through, what with Ella being past forty and her husband being, well, not the sharpest knife in the drawer. Somehow they'd passed all the tests, though, and met all the requirements for adoption. Martha Lee was quite sure it was due to her extra prayers. Big Al hadn't a clue how it had happened; he was just glad it had. Now they were bringing little Sarah Jane to meet her grandparents for the first time. The other Tanner children and grandchildren would be there too, so Martha Lee had already asked Big Al to bring the extra card table down from the attic so she could set it up for the overflow from the dining room.

Big, loud, family get-togethers mattered to Big Al, as he had been an only child with just the one first cousin, Dudley. Big Al doesn't mean to speak out of turn, but he feels Dudley hasn't lived up to his potential, or maybe he never had any to start with. After Dudley called for a second time in the middle of the night requesting bail money, Big Al had put his foot down. They hadn't spoken since.

The holidays of Big Al's youth were always understated affairs, with everything over and done by one in the afternoon on Thanksgiving and Christmas. That was the main reason Big Al insisted on having four children; he wanted the home of his adulthood to be filled with noise and laughter and love. He didn't even mind occasional bickering because it makes him feel alive to have so much activity in the house.

This year Big Al decided a change was in order, what with all the excitement about the new baby. Instead of having ham and quail, Big Al would fry a turkey. He'd already talked to Joe down at Luckettville Hardware and Sundries about what equipment he needed.

Martha Lee would handle the side dishes, as she was known far and wide for her broccoli casserole and tomato aspic. The daughters would provide dessert. Mary Ellen always brought her gingerbread with lemon sauce, while Ella liked to make jam cakes. Mandy had a flair for fruit cocktail cake, a family tradition that started when Big Al told a story about never getting to eat fruit cocktail as a kid because his father, a devout deacon in the Holy Faithfulness All Gospel Chapel, wouldn't allow anything in the house with the word cocktail in it. It sounds severe, or maybe even made up, but it's the truth.

Martha Lee always cries during the blessing, and this year is no different. All her life she's been accused of being "too sensitive," and she used to let that get to her. But once she hit her sixties, Martha Lee had decided to be herself no matter what. So when Big Al stands at the head of the table and thanks God for their beautiful children and the bounty spread out before them, Martha Lee sniffles into her linen handkerchief without apology.

But soon she is crying for real. Just as the Tanners start passing the strawberry butter and persimmon bread, they hear a loud boom, followed by pieces of the shed flying past the camellia bushes in the side yard. Turns out Big Al left the fryer on, and all that hot grease had nowhere to go but up and out. No one is hurt, though, and the Tanners add that to their list of things to be thankful for.

After the firemen have gone—Martha Lee packed them some food for the firehouse—the Tanners spend most of the afternoon telling stories and sharing memories. Like the time Big Al reported his car stolen, only to locate it on the other side of the mall an hour later right where he had parked it. Or when Mandy woke up to see Big Al riding her new bike toward their house from a neighbor's, thereby shattering her long-held belief in Santa Claus without so much as a warning.

"He looked like some sort of middle-aged clown," she says, "riding that banana bike in his pajamas, his knees sticking out on each side. He didn't even put on a robe."

"I overslept," says Big Al. "You kids always woke up so early on Christmas Day that I didn't have time."

"It was exactly what I wanted." Mandy smiles.

They pull out tales they've all heard many times before, repeated so often that even the sons-in-law know the punch lines. It doesn't matter. What matters is that they are together, there is a new baby in their midst, and insurance should cover the shed.

Sour Cream Blueberry Pancakes with Cinnamon Honey Syrup

The holidays are the perfect time for a family pancake breakfast. This recipe is delicious, and you will love the syrup.

Pancakes
2 cups milk
2 large eggs, lightly beaten
1 (8-ounce) carton sour cream
2 cups all-purpose flour
2 tablespoons baking powder
2 tablespoons sugar
1/2 teaspoon salt
1/4 cup butter, melted
1 1/2 cups fresh blueberries

Cinnamon Honey Syrup
1 cup brown sugar
1 cup sugar
1 cup water
1 cup honey
1 teaspoon cinnamon
1/2 teaspoon maple flavoring

To make the pancakes: In a large bowl, combine the milk, eggs, and sour cream, and mix well. In a medium bowl, mix together the flour, baking powder, sugar, and salt. Add to the milk mixture. Mix until smooth. Stir in the butter, and fold in the blueberries.

Preheat an iron skillet over medium heat. Pour 1/4 cup of the batter onto a hot and lightly greased skillet. When bubbles form on the top, the pancake is ready to turn, about 2 minutes per side.

To make the syrup: Combine the brown sugar, sugar, and water in a medium saucepan, and bring to a boil. Let boil for 1 minute. Remove from the heat, and add the honey, cinnamon, and maple flavoring.

Makes 6 servings

Note: If you're using an electric griddle, preheat to 375 degrees.

CHOCOLATE CANDY NUT CLUSTERS

These are so good for a Christmas candy tray or any party you are having.

1 pound vanilla candy coating
1/2 pound chocolate candy coating
2 ounces German chocolate
1 cup semi-sweet chocolate chips
1 pound roasted and salted peanuts
8 ounces cashew halves
1/2 teaspoon vanilla extract

Turn your slow cooker to high heat. Spray the container with non-stick pan spray.

Add the vanilla bar, chocolate bar, German chocolate, chocolate chips, peanuts, and cashew halves. Place the lid on, and cook 45 minutes. Do not lift the lid or stir. Reduce the heat to low, and cook 1 hour. Remove the lid and stir until all the chocolate is incorporated. Add the vanilla, mixing well. Dip by tablespoons into miniature paper liners. Allow to harden at room temperature. Store covered in an airtight container.

Makes 60 servings

Miss Vara's Cherry-Berry Jam Cake with Caramel Icing

This recipe came from Miss Vara Powers, who was not only my next door neighbor but also my son's second-grade teacher. When I make this recipe, I always think of her and what a wonderful person she was.

Cake

1 1/2 cups sugar
1/2 cup shortening
3 large eggs
1 teaspoon allspice
2 teaspoons cinnamon
1 teaspoon cloves
1 teaspoon nutmeg
1 1/2 teaspoons cocoa
1/2 teaspoon salt
2 1/2 cups self-rising flour
1 1/4 teaspoons baking soda
1 1/2 cups buttermilk
1 teaspoon vanilla extract

1 cup cherry preserves
1 cup blackberry jam
1/2 cup applesauce
1 cup raisins
1 cup pecans, chopped

Caramel Icing

1/2 cup heavy whipping cream
1/2 cup butter
1 teaspoon vanilla extract
1 pound brown sugar
1/2 teaspoon salt
1/2 cup powdered sugar

To make the cake: Preheat the oven to 350 degrees. Grease and flour three 9-inch cake pans.

In a large bowl, cream the sugar and shortening with an electric mixer. Add the eggs one at a time. In a separate bowl, mix together the allspice, cinnamon, cloves, nutmeg, cocoa, salt, and self-rising flour. Set aside. Combine the baking soda and buttermilk in a small bowl, and add alternately with the dry ingredients to the creamed mixture. Mix well. Add the vanilla, cherry preserves, blackberry jam, applesauce, raisins, and pecans. Blend well. Divide between the cake pans, and bake 25 to 30 minutes, or until a toothpick inserted in the center comes out clean. Cool before icing.

To make the icing: Place the cream, butter, vanilla, brown sugar, and salt together in a medium saucepan. Bring to a boil, stirring constantly for 1 1/2 minutes. Remove from the heat and blend in the powdered sugar.

To assemble: Place one cake on a plate and spread the caramel icing over the top. Place the second cake on top, and ice the top and sides. Store leftovers covered at room temperature or wrap tightly in plastic wrap and freeze.

Makes 16 servings

Strawberry Butter

You can eat this on biscuits, waffles, pound cake, or even bagels.

1 cup butter, softened
1 cup fresh strawberries, coarsely chopped
1/2 cup sugar
1 teaspoon vanilla extract

Mix the butter, strawberries, sugar, and vanilla in the bowl of a food processor. Blend at high speed 2 minutes or until the ingredients are mixed well. Place in a covered container and store in the refrigerator. May be made up to 4 days ahead.

Makes 2 cups

Niva's Pralines

Niva Martin gave piano lessons to both of my children. She also taught a lot of people where I live how to make candy. I still have the handwritten recipe she gave me for this, even though she has been gone for more than twenty-five years.

2 cups sugar
1 cup milk
8 large marshmallows
2 tablespoons butter
1/2 teaspoon vanilla extract
2 cups pecan halves

Butter one 24-inch piece of wax paper. Combine the sugar, milk, and marshmallows in a heavy 4-quart saucepan. Cook over medium heat to a soft ball stage (234 degrees), stirring constantly. Remove from the heat, and stir in the butter, vanilla, and pecans. Beat just until the mixture begins to thicken. Working rapidly, drop by tablespoons onto the prepared wax paper. Cool and store in an airtight container.

Makes 15 to 18 (3-inch) pralines

SaRa's PeaNUT BRITTLE

When I hear my dear friend Sara Caudill talk about buying large amounts of peanuts, my mouth waters because I know it's peanut brittle time.

3 cups raw peanuts, shelled
2 cups sugar
1 cup light corn syrup
1/2 cup water
1/4 cup butter
1 1/2 teaspoons baking soda

Preheat the oven to 350 degrees. Butter 2 large shallow pans. Spread the peanuts evenly in the pan in a single layer. Bake 16 minutes. Stir the peanuts two times as they are roasting. (The peanuts will begin to split and crackle.) At the same time the peanuts go into the oven, put the sugar, corn syrup, and water into a heavy medium saucepan. Cook on high heat until it comes to a boil. Reduce to medium, and cook the syrup until it reaches 300 degrees on a candy thermometer.

Stir the peanuts into the syrup until they are well coated. Add the butter, stirring until it melts. Add the baking soda, and stir until the mixture is foaming. Pour the hot mixture into the buttered pans, and spread it into a thin, even layer. Let cool, and then break into small pieces. Store in an airtight container.

Makes 2 pounds

PERSIMMON BREAD

Persimmons are about as abundant as kudzu in the South. But if you are going to use the fruit off the tree, wait until after the first frost. Otherwise, rely on the ones you find in the grocery store.

3 3/4 cups all-purpose flour
2 teaspoons baking soda
1 teaspoon salt
2 1/2 cups sugar
1/2 teaspoon allspice
1 teaspoon cinnamon
1 cup butter, melted
4 large eggs, beaten
2/3 cup orange juice
2 cups persimmon pulp (4 or 5 medium)
1 cup pecans, chopped
1 1/2 cups raisins
1 (8 ounce) package cream cheese, softened (optional)

Preheat the oven to 350 degrees. Grease and flour two 9 x 5-inch loaf pans.

In a large bowl, sift together the flour, baking soda, salt, sugar, allspice, and cinnamon. Reserve 1/2 cup of the dry ingredients to dredge the pecans and raisins in. In a small bowl, combine the butter, eggs, orange juice, and persimmon pulp. Add to the dry mix. Mix until smooth. Add the pecans and raisins to the reserved dry mix and then stir into the batter. Divide the batter between the loaf pans.

Bake 1 hour, or until a cake tester inserted in the center comes out clean. Cool before removing from the pans. To serve, slice and eat plain or spread with softened cream cheese.

Makes 2 loaves

Note: This could also be baked in a tube pan.

FRUIT COCKTAIL CAKE

This is a cake I have been serving for more than fifty years. When something isn't broken, there is no need to fix it.

Cake

2 cups all-purpose flour
1 1/2 cups sugar
2 teaspoons baking soda
1/2 teaspoon salt
1 (15-ounce) can fruit cocktail
2 large eggs, beaten
1 teaspoon vanilla extract

Icing

1 cup evaporated milk
3/4 cup butter
1 1/2 cups sugar
1 teaspoon vanilla extract
1 cup flaked coconut
1/2 cup pecans, chopped

To make the cake: Preheat the oven to 350 degrees. Grease and flour a 13 x 9-inch baking pan.

Combine the flour, sugar, baking soda, and salt in a large mixing bowl. Stir in the fruit cocktail, eggs, and vanilla. Pour into the prepared pan. Bake 30 to 35 minutes, or until golden brown and a toothpick inserted in the center comes out clean.

To make the icing: Combine the milk, butter, and sugar in a small saucepan. Cook over medium heat until the mixture boils. Boil 2 minutes, stirring constantly. Remove from the heat, and add the vanilla, coconut, and pecans. Spread over the cake. Cut into squares and serve. Store leftovers covered at room temperature.

Makes 12 servings

CARROT CAKE WITH CREAM CHEESE ICING

One reason I like this cake is because it's a simple, one-layer cake. Just bake it, ice it, and enjoy it.

Cake

3 cups self-rising flour

2 cups sugar

1 teaspoon cinnamon

1 1/2 cups vegetable oil

4 large eggs, slightly beaten

2 cups carrots, grated (2 medium)

1 cup pecans, chopped

Cream Cheese Icing

1 (8-ounce) package cream cheese, softened

1/2 cup butter, softened

1 pound powdered sugar

1 teaspoon vanilla extract

To make the cake: Preheat the oven to 325 degrees. Grease and flour a 10-inch tube or Bundt pan.

Combine the flour, sugar, and cinnamon in a large bowl. Stir in the oil. Mix in the beaten eggs, carrots, and pecans. Pour the mixture into the prepared pan, and bake 1 hour. Cool 10 minutes before removing from the pan. Cool completely before icing.

To make the icing: In a medium bowl, mix the cream cheese and butter. Beat in the powdered sugar and vanilla. Ice the top and sides of the cake. Keep refrigerated.

Makes 16 servings

Honey Peanut Butter Topping

This is great on toast or banana bread.

$^1/_4$ cup butter, softened
$^1/_4$ cup creamy peanut butter
$^1/_2$ cup powdered sugar
$^1/_3$ cup honey
$^1/_4$ teaspoon cinnamon

Cream the butter and peanut butter in a mixing bowl, using an electric mixer on medium speed. Add the powdered sugar, honey, and cinnamon, beating until blended. Keep refrigerated.

Makes 1 cup

Coconut Chocolate Buckeyes

When I was growing up, these were a staple in our house at Christmastime.

1 (14-ounce) package flaked coconut
2 pounds powdered sugar
$^1/_2$ cup butter, melted
1 (14-ounce) can sweetened condensed milk
1 teaspoon vanilla extract
1 (11-ounce) bag milk chocolate chips
2 tablespoons paraffin or vegetable shortening

Place the coconut in a large mixing bowl. Add the powdered sugar, butter, condensed milk, and vanilla. Stir to mix well. Form into small balls, about 1 $^1/_2$ inches in diameter. Place on a tray, cover, and refrigerate.

Melt the chocolate chips and paraffin in a double boiler over hot water, stirring until the chocolate is melted. To coat the coconut balls, drop a few at a time into the melted chocolate, using a spoon to coat evenly. Place the balls on waxed paper to cool. When completely cool, place them in a sealed container and store in a cool place.

Makes 96 buckeyes

PUMPKIN PIE

While fresh pumpkin is readily available during the holidays, I have always used canned for this recipe. But if you have the time, fresh would be delicious too.

1 (15-ounce) can pumpkin or 2 cups freshly cooked and mashed
1 (14-ounce) can sweetened condensed milk
1 large egg, beaten
$1/2$ teaspoon salt
$1/2$ teaspoon cinnamon
$1/4$ teaspoon nutmeg
$1/4$ teaspoon ginger
$1/8$ teaspoon cloves
1 cup hot water
1 (9 inch) pie shell, unbaked
Whipped cream for garnish (optional)

Preheat the oven to 375 degrees. In a medium bowl, combine the pumpkin, condensed milk, egg, salt, cinnamon, nutmeg, ginger, cloves, and water. Whisk to blend the ingredients together. Pour into the pie shell, and bake 50 to 55 minutes, or until a knife inserted in the center comes out clean. Cool slightly.

This is best served at room temperature. Garnish with whipped cream, if desired.

Makes 6 to 8 servings

PUMPKIN CAKE WITH CREAM CHEESE ICING

This is the perfect addition to any holiday table.

Cake

2 cups sugar

1 (15-ounce) can pure pumpkin

1 cup vegetable oil

4 large eggs, beaten

2 cups all-purpose flour

1 teaspoon salt

2 teaspoons baking soda

2 teaspoons baking powder

2 teaspoons cinnamon

1/2 cup flaked coconut

3/4 cup pecans, chopped

Cream Cheese Icing

1/2 cup butter, softened

1 (8-ounce) package cream cheese, softened

1 pound powdered sugar

2 teaspoons vanilla extract

1/2 cup pecans, chopped

1/2 cup flaked coconut

To make the cake: Preheat the oven to 350 degrees. Grease and flour three 8-inch cake pans.

Combine the sugar, pumpkin, oil, and eggs in the bowl of an electric mixer. Beat at medium speed for 1 minute. In a medium bowl, combine the flour, salt, baking soda, baking powder, and cinnamon. Add the flour mixture to the pumpkin mixture, and beat for 1 minute. Stir in the coconut and pecans. Divide the batter among the three cake pans.

Bake 25 to 30 minutes, or until a cake tester inserted in the center comes out clean. Cool in the pans for 10 minutes. Remove from the pans and cool completely.

To make the icing: In a large bowl, combine the butter and cream cheese with an electric mixer. Beat in the powdered sugar and vanilla. Stir in the pecans and coconut.

To assemble: Place one cake on a plate, and spread a thin layer of icing on top. Place the second cake on top of the first, and spread another thin layer of icing. Place the third cake on top, and ice the top and sides of the cakes. Cover and refrigerate leftovers.

Makes 16 servings

Tess's Divinity

My sister Tess is known far and wide for this divinity. She says you can't make this on a rainy day, though. So check the weather forecast first.

1/2 cup water
1/2 cup light corn syrup
2 cups sugar
2 large egg whites at room temperature
1 teaspoon vanilla extract
1 cup pecans, coarsely chopped

Place the water and corn syrup into a medium saucepan. Add the sugar and stir to dissolve. Cover the pan and place over medium heat. Bring to a boil. Cook about 3 minutes. Remove the cover, and continue to cook, without stirring, until you reach the hard ball stage (254 degrees).

While the syrup is cooking, place the egg whites in a large bowl and beat with an electric mixer at medium speed until they are stiff enough to hold their shape. When the syrup has reached the cooked stage, begin pouring it over the beaten egg whites in a fine stream, beating at high speed. Add the vanilla. Change to a large spoon to continue beating. Add the chopped nuts.

When the candy is thick and creamy and holds its shape, drop by teaspoonfuls onto waxed paper. Store in an airtight container.

Makes 24 pieces

FRUIT CAKE COOKIES

Christmas in a cookie.

1 cup brown sugar
1/4 cup butter, softened
4 large eggs, well beaten
1/2 cup peach brandy
3 tablespoons milk
1 teaspoon baking soda
3 1/4 cups all-purpose flour, divided
1 teaspoon cinnamon
1 teaspoon nutmeg
1 teaspoon allspice
1 1/4 pounds candied cherries
1 1/4 pounds candied pineapple
1 1/2 pounds pecan halves

Preheat the oven to 350 degrees. Grease a large cookie sheet.

In a large bowl, cream the sugar and butter together with a spoon. Add the well-beaten eggs and brandy. Combine the milk and baking soda in a small bowl, and stir to dissolve. In a large bowl, sift together 3 cups of flour, cinnamon, nutmeg, and allspice. Alternately add the flour mixture and the milk to the batter, stirring with a spoon. Dredge the cherries, pineapple, and pecan halves in the remaining 1/4 cup flour. Add the fruit and pecans to the batter, stirring to combine.

Drop by tablespoonfuls onto the prepared pan. Bake 12 minutes. Cool and store in an airtight container.

Makes 72 cookies

GINGERBREAD WITH LEMON SAUCE

We had a molasses mill on our farm when I was growing up. Gingerbread was a fall staple at our house because we had the molasses we made. This bread smells as good as it tastes.

Gingerbread

3 large eggs, slightly beaten

1 cup sugar

1 cup vegetable oil

1 cup molasses

1 teaspoon ground cloves

1 teaspoon ginger

1 teaspoon cinnamon

$1/2$ teaspoon salt

2 teaspoons baking soda

2 tablespoons hot water

2 cups all-purpose flour

1 cup boiling water

Lemon Sauce

1 cup sugar

2 tablespoons cornstarch

2 cups boiling water

$1/4$ cup butter

$1/4$ cup lemon juice

1 teaspoon grated lemon zest

To make the bread: Preheat the oven to 375 degrees. Grease and flour a 13 x 9-inch baking pan.

In a large bowl, mix together the eggs, sugar, oil, and molasses. Stir in the cloves, ginger, cinnamon, and salt, and beat well. In a small bowl, dissolve the baking soda in the hot water, and add it to the beaten mixture. Stir in the flour, and continue to beat well. Add the boiling water, beating quickly. Pour the batter into the prepared pan. Bake 45 minutes.

To make the sauce: Mix the sugar and cornstarch together in a medium saucepan. Add the boiling water, whisking constantly. Place on medium heat, and bring to a boil. Continue to cook, stirring constantly, about 3 minutes or until the sauce is thick and clear. Remove from the heat, and add the butter, lemon juice, and zest. Serve warm over the gingerbread.

Makes 12 servings

THREE-TIMES-THE-COCONUT CAKE WITH DIVINITY ICING

I call this cake Three Times the Coconut because it uses cream of coconut in the cake, frozen coconut in the filling, and toasted coconut on top. Heaven for coconut lovers.

Cake

2 1/2 cups all-purpose flour
2 1/2 teaspoons baking powder
1/2 teaspoon baking soda
1/2 teaspoon salt
1 cup butter, softened
1 1/2 cups sugar
1 cup canned sweetened cream of coconut
4 large eggs
2 teaspoons vanilla extract
1 cup milk

Filling

1 cup sour cream
2 cups sugar
3 (6-ounce) packages frozen coconut

Toasted Coconut

3 cups flaked coconut

Divinity Icing

3 large egg whites
3/4 cup sugar
1/3 cup light corn syrup
1/4 teaspoon cream of tartar

To make the cake: Preheat the oven to 350 degrees. Grease and flour two 9-inch cake pans.

In a large bowl, sift the flour, baking powder, baking soda, and salt together. Set aside. Beat the butter, sugar, and cream of coconut together in a large bowl with an electric mixer on low speed until blended. Add the eggs and vanilla. Add the flour mixture and milk to the batter, and beat at low speed until mixed. Divide the batter equally between the prepared pans.

Bake 35 to 40 minutes, or until a toothpick inserted in the center comes out clean. Cool 10 minutes. Turn out onto a rack to cool completely. Slice each layer horizontally to make 4 layers.
To make the filling: In a medium bowl, mix together the sour cream, sugar, and coconut. Keep refrigerated, stirring occasionally to dissolve the sugar.
To make the toasted coconut: Preheat the oven to 300 degrees. Spread the coconut on a large cookie sheet. Toast 10 minutes or until the coconut is golden brown, stirring occasionally. Cool.
To make the icing: Place the egg whites, sugar, corn syrup, and cream of tartar into the top of a double boiler over hot water. Beat constantly with an electric mixer at high speed. Continue to beat 7 to 10 minutes, or until the mixture is a spreading consistency. Remove the double boiler from the heat.

To assemble: Place half of a cake on a plate, cut side up. Spread $1/3$ of the filling over the layer. Top with the second half of the cake, cut side up, and repeat with the filling. Continue to do this until you have only one cake half remaining. Place the final cake half cut side down. Spread the divinity icing over the top and sides of the cake. Sprinkle the toasted coconut over the top and sides of the cake.

Makes 16 servings

DEVIL'S FOOD PEPPERMINT ICE CREAM CAKE

I love the combination of peppermint and chocolate. This cake is beautiful to look at and delicious to eat.

1 (18.25-ounce) devil's food cake mix, plus box ingredients to make the cake
1 $1/2$ quarts peppermint ice cream
1 (12-ounce) container frozen whipped topping, thawed
1 cup peppermint candy, crushed, for garnish

Preheat the oven to 350 degrees. Grease and flour three 9-inch cake pans.

Mix and bake the cake according to the package directions. Cool 10 minutes in the pan. Turn out onto wire racks to cool completely.

To assemble, soften the ice cream. Place one cake on a plate, and spread half the ice cream on top. Add the second cake and the remaining ice cream. Top with the third layer of cake, cover, and place in the freezer for 6 hours or longer.

Remove the frozen cake, and ice with the thawed whipped topping. Garnish with the crushed peppermint candy. Keep frozen until ready to serve. Soften in the refrigerator for 10 minutes before serving. Cut with a knife that has been dipped in hot water.

Makes 16 servings

Jam Cake

This jam cake is easier than most traditional jam cakes because it has only one layer. But the same delicious taste.

Cake

2 cups all-purpose flour
1 teaspoon salt
1 teaspoon baking soda
1 teaspoon cinnamon
1 teaspoon nutmeg
1 teaspoon allspice
3 large eggs, beaten
1 1/2 cups sugar
1 cup vegetable oil
1 cup buttermilk

1 cup pecans, chopped
1 cup blackberry jam
1 teaspoon vanilla extract

Icing

1 1/2 cups sugar
3/4 cup butter
3/4 cup buttermilk
3/4 teaspoon baking soda
2 tablespoons light corn syrup

To make the cake: Preheat the oven to 325 degrees. Grease and flour a 13 x 9-inch baking pan.

In a medium bowl, sift together the flour, salt, baking soda, cinnamon, nutmeg, and allspice. Set aside. In a large bowl, whisk together the eggs and sugar. Add the oil, and stir to combine. Alternately add the dry mixture and the buttermilk to the egg mixture. Stir in the pecans, jam, and vanilla. Pour the batter into the baking pan, and bake 40 to 45 minutes, or until a toothpick inserted in the center comes out clean.

To make the icing: Mix the sugar, butter, buttermilk, baking soda, and corn syrup together in a medium saucepan. Place over medium heat, and bring to a boil. Boil 3 minutes, stirring occasionally. Let cool 5 minutes, and beat with a wooden spoon until it reaches a spreadable consistency. Spread the icing over the warm cake.

Makes 12 to 16 servings

FRENCH TOAST FINGERS WITH ORANGE SAUCE

In the South, the color orange can get you in trouble. The University of Tennessee is one color orange. My nephew goes to Auburn, and their school color is another shade of orange. But this is one orange that everyone can agree on.

French Toast Fingers

Oil for frying
8 slices white bread
1 cup all-purpose flour
1 tablespoon sugar
1 1/2 teaspoons baking powder
1/2 teaspoon salt
1/2 teaspoon cinnamon
1 cup milk
1 large egg, slightly beaten

Orange Sauce

1 tablespoon cornstarch
1/2 cup sugar
1/4 teaspoon salt
1/4 teaspoon cinnamon
1 cup orange juice
1 teaspoon grated orange zest
1 tablespoon butter
1 orange, peeled, sectioned, and diced

To make the French toast: Preheat your deep fryer to 375 degrees. Slice each bread slice into 4 pieces (fingers). Mix the flour, sugar, baking powder, salt, and cinnamon in a medium mixing bowl. In a small bowl, combine the milk and egg. Add the wet to the dry ingredients, and mix until smooth.

Dip each finger of bread into the batter. Fry until golden brown, about 1 minute per side. Drain on paper towels. Serve hot with the orange sauce.

To make the sauce: Mix the cornstarch, sugar, salt, and cinnamon together in a small saucepan. Stir in the orange juice and zest. Cook over medium heat until it comes to a boil, stirring constantly. Add the butter and orange sections. Mix well.

Makes 4 to 6 servings

sweet Potato Pie with Praline Topping

If you want your sweet potato pie to stand out in front of the others this Thanksgiving, serve this version with the praline topping.

Pie

2 medium sweet potatoes (1 pound)
$\frac{1}{4}$ cup butter
1 cup brown sugar
1 teaspoon cinnamon
2 large eggs, slightly beaten
$\frac{1}{2}$ cup light whipping cream
1 (9-inch) pie shell, unbaked

Praline Topping

3 tablespoons brown sugar
3 tablespoons light corn syrup
1 tablespoon butter
$\frac{1}{2}$ teaspoon vanilla extract
$\frac{3}{4}$ cup pecans, chopped

To make the pie: Preheat the oven to 350 degrees. Peel and slice the potatoes. Place the slices in a medium saucepan and cover with water. Cook approximately 20 minutes. Drain and mash. You should have 2 cups.

Add the butter, brown sugar, cinnamon, eggs, and cream to the mashed sweet potatoes. Pour the sweet potato mixture into the pie shell. Bake 30 minutes.

To make the topping: Combine the brown sugar, corn syrup, and butter in a small saucepan. Cook over medium heat. Bring to a boil, stirring constantly for 2 minutes. Add the vanilla and pecans. Spoon the praline topping over the pie, and cook an additional 20 minutes, or until a knife inserted in the center comes out clean.

Makes 6 to 8 servings

CHRISTMAS PEPPERMINT BARK

This will disappear quicker than you think at Christmastime. I always make a double batch.

1 (11.5-ounce) bag milk chocolate chips
1 (11.5-ounce) bag white chocolate chips
1 teaspoon vegetable shortening
$^1/_2$ cup peppermint candy, crushed
$^1/_2$ cup pistachio nuts, chopped (optional)
$^1/_2$ cup dried cranberries, chopped (optional)

Cover a large cookie sheet with parchment paper. Melt the milk chocolate chips in a microwave-safe bowl, stirring every 15 seconds until the chips have completely melted. Spread the chocolate evenly over the parchment paper to form a 12-inch square. Place the pan in the refrigerator for 30 minutes, or until the layer is firm.

Melt the white chocolate chips in a microwave-safe bowl, stirring every 15 seconds until the chips are melted. Stir in the shortening (this makes for better spreading consistency). Spread the white chocolate over the cooled chocolate layer. Sprinkle with crushed candy, pistachios, and cranberries, pressing them into the white chocolate layer. Refrigerate 30 minutes, or until firm. Break into pieces and store in an airtight container. If you have leftovers, you can freeze them.

Makes 1 $^1/_2$ pounds

ACKNOWLEDGMENTS

Just as I heard "You be sweet" from my own dear mother, Irene Foster, growing up, I subject my own children and now grandchildren to this phrase on a frequent basis. I have been lucky enough to have many sweet people in my own life who have influenced both this book and me.

My son, Bryan Curtis, and my daughter, Kelly Sims, have provided support and encouragement, along with a dose of "Do you remember's?" about desserts I used to make them when they were children that I had no idea they would remember. Some of those "do you remember" desserts are in this book. I am also grateful to my son-in-law, Randy, and my grandchildren, Scott and Paige, for their love and healthy appetites.

This book wouldn't be possible without my husband, Bill Caldwell, who was happy to give me his opinion on every item in this book or to jump in his truck and run to the grocery store when I needed something right away to finish one of these desserts or deliver something to the many tasters I have around my hometown, Charlotte, Tennessee.

I would also like to thank Heather Skelton, Joel Miller, Mindy Henderson, and everyone at Thomas Nelson for their support of this project. To Ron Manville and Teresa Blackburn, thank you for making the book and my food look so beautiful.

To Amy Lyles Wilson, I am so honored that my recipes have found a home with your wonderful stories. I think they go together like peanut butter and chocolate.

The best compliment any cook can receive is when someone asks for seconds. I am so fortunate to have many friends who have supported our first book, *Bless Your Heart: Saving the World One Covered Dish at a Time*. It is because of those friends and all the people who purchased the first book that this second book exists. My heartfelt thanks go out to the people of Ingram Industries, the people of Dickson County, Phillip and Marie Wallace, Gayle Knickerbocker, the Fowler family, Sue Harvey, Luanne Greer, and Johnny Chandler.

And last, but certainly not least, this book wouldn't be possible without my ladies in the Water Tower cooking class: Donna Brown, Sue Drinnen, Betsy Duke, Cynthia Marvin, Judy Nicks, Judy Redden, Betty Nicks Smith, Sue Smith, Gay Taylor, and Sara Caudill.

PATSY CALDWELL

With heartfelt thanks to those who helped make this book possible, including Patsy Caldwell, cook extraordinaire; idea man Bryan Curtis; Martha Grace Gray and Mary-Milam Granberry, my lifelines to the younger generation; Kim Green and Maryglenn McCombs, for hearing me out and spurring me on; editor Heather Skelton and the entire Thomas Nelson publishing team; and the countless storytellers who surround me, past and present.

AMY LYLES WILSON

INDEX